Ultimate Authority for the Soul

Martin Murphy

To

The Church

Acknowledgments

The Word of God often referred to as Holy Scripture or the Bible provided me the point of reference for understanding truth. I am a rational being and the pursuit of truth is my passion in life. As unbelievable as Holy Scripture is, the Holy Spirit has enabled me to understand it, so I could believe it. I am unable to express the thanks and gratitude for such a noble and dignified gift. The ability to believe the unbelievable is the fullest accomplishment in this life. God sent godly men to help me in my pursuit for truth. The names are too many to list, but I must acknowledge the importance of each one that made my journey sensible.

Preface

Someone may have the power to commit crimes, but that same person does not have the authority to violate the law. The words "power" and "authority" are often misused. Authority delegates power and instrumentation to make critical judgment and issue orders for enforcement. For example, the police officer has the authority to issue citations to appear before a judge. The authority given to the local judge is to decide guilt or innocence of the alleged criminal. An appeal may be made to a higher court that has authority over the lower court. The authority given to the judge is from a body of legislators. Everyone is under the authority of someone else. The continuity of authority is in the document established by the person or persons of a higher authority. Every culture in human history has various levels and degrees of authority, because there is no ultimate authority.

Christians enjoy the security and comfort of having an ultimate authority. God is the ultimate authority. God's people have the privilege of understanding the ultimate, perfect, and just authority, because God has made it available in the Word of God. Like an inspired and infallible constitution, the Word of God is the ultimate authority for the soul.

Table of Contents

1. By What Authority 1

2. The Blessed Man 7

3. Ultimate Authority for Young People 13

4. Open My Eyes 19

5. Understand God's Truth... 25

6. Spiritual Discernment 31

7. Mercy With Truth 37

8. Relief From Ridicule 43

9. Life After Conversion.. 51

10. The Real is not Deceptive....................................... 57

11. Prayer According to God's Word................................. 63

12. Secular Life.. 69

13. God Does Not Mutate 75

14. Sound Understanding.. 81

15. The Center of Life 87

16. Hate One, Love the Other 93

17. Servant in a Sinful World 99

18. Passionate Christian.. 105

19. Whose Justice? Which Life? 111

20. Divine Proximity 117

21. Spiritual Maturity.. 123

22. Great Peace From God's Word 129

23. Authority of God's Word 135

1. By What Authority

Now it happened on one of those days, as He taught the people in the temple and preached the gospel, that the chief priests and the scribes, together with the elders, confronted Him and spoke to Him, saying, "Tell us, by what authority are You doing these things? Or who is he who gave You this authority?" But He answered and said to them, "I also will ask you one thing, and answer Me: The baptism of John—was it from heaven or from men?" And they reasoned among themselves, saying, "If we say, 'From heaven,' He will say, 'Why then did you not believe him?' But if we say, 'From men,' all the people will stone us, for they are persuaded that John was a prophet." So they answered that they did not know where it was from. And Jesus said to them, "Neither will I tell you by what authority I do these things."

Luke 20:1-26

The principles necessary to maintain sanity and order in any society are basic and fundamental. For instance, the family is essential to any larger society. Authority is a principle necessary to maintain sanity and order in the family. The question for every Christian is, "What is authority and what is its source?"

Black's Law Dictionary describes authority as, "power delegated by a principal to his agent." The distinction must be made between power and authority. Power refers to the ability to perform some action. One army is more powerful than the other. Authority enables the power to act. The Greek word *exousia* frequently used in the New Testament refers to absolute authority. The Army officer has proximate authority over his troops, but all ultimate authority is from God. Christians believe the Bible is the ultimate authority from God. It is the regulative principle for Christians. The regulative principle was the term used by the Puritans to describe their appeal to God's authority. The truth from the mind of God is the regulative principle for all Christians. The author of the regulative principle is God. It is the standard by which Christians measure what they believe and how they obey God.

One day while Jesus was teaching in the Temple and preaching the gospel, the chief priests, scribes and elders confronted Jesus with these questions, "By what authority are you doing these things? Or who is he who gave You this authority?" (Luke 20:2).

The priests, scribes, and elders were religious leaders, but the Bible describes the majority of them as mean-spirited, hard-hearted unbelievers. Jesus was probably teaching the law of God to show them the need for a Savior and teaching the gospel to show them the way of salvation. Their questions about His source of authority to teach and preach stigmatized their fear because they knew the answer (Luke 20:5-7).

When Jesus began His teaching ministry the people were astonished because His words were with authority (Luke 4:32). When Jesus healed the sick and forgave their sins, the church leaders questioned His authority (Luke 5:22-24). Jesus gave His disciples authority over demons and authority to cure diseases. It was the authority of Jesus that was held in contempt by many who heard His teaching and preaching. His miracles demonstrated his authority and that frustrated them all the more.

The chief priests, the scribes, and the elders demonstrated contempt for the authority of Jesus Christ, the second person of the Trinity. The painful question that every Christian must answer is, "do I demonstrate contempt for God's authority?" A serious inquiry may reveal several ways that Christians slight God's authority. First, the sin nature will cause Christians to disincline themselves from God's authority and incline themselves toward self-authority. Christians must also realize the Word of God, the full counsel of God, is the ultimate authority for the Christian life. When Jesus appeared to His disciples on the road to Emmaus (Luke 24:13-45), He referred to the full counsel of God in terms of, "the Law of Moses and the Prophets and the Psalms" (Luke 24:44). Jesus "opened their understanding, that they might comprehend the Scriptures" (Luke 24:45; John 8:42-47).

Authority translates into power and power translates into control. If Christians understand God's authority correctly, they will have power to minister according to His Word. If the authority is fraudulent, the power is ungodly. Even Satan had power, but he did not have authority to exercise his power.

If the religious leaders could show the people that Jesus did not have ultimate authority, then the people would lose respect for Jesus. It is called mind control. It is one of the most powerful forces in the world. Jim Jones convinced a multitude of people to drink poison by mind control. David Koresh convinced people to burn to death with him by mind control. Adolph Hitler captivated the minds of the German people. These men were deluded by proximate authority. The here and the now was all that was important. They couldn't see the concept of ultimate authority which is nothing less that divine authority. Words are the primary means used to usurp authority. The serpent said to the woman: "You will not surely die." Satan's charm and mind control captivated the woman. It was a contest with words. Did God mean what he said or did He mean something else? It was the words of Jesus that captivated the people and the wicked church leaders hated His words and that caused them to hate the man Jesus and that caused them to question His authority.

Jesus answered the Jewish religious leaders with a parable (Luke 20:9-19). In this parable Jesus described some tenants (share-croppers) who refused to pay proper respect to the owner. They were unwilling to share the profits with the owner. They tried to gain possession of his property by murdering the owner's representatives and eventually the owner's son. Their contempt of authority caused them to act irrationally. When it was time for the owner to collect his legal and rightful share, he sent a messenger to collect the money. The share-croppers rejected the authority given to the messenger. The owner sent messengers three times to collect his portion of the profits. The messengers were abused and beaten by the tenants. The tenants rejected the authority of the three messengers. There is an analogy between this and the parable of the rich man and Lazarus. The man in Hell said, "send Lazarus to warn my brothers." He deceives himself with the idea that he still has proximate authority. But Abraham said, "They have Moses and the prophets; let them hear them." Moses gave the the law of God to teach the need for the gospel. It was also given as a moral regulative principle. The history of the Old Testament is a sad story, because many of the professing people of God repudiated the authority of Scripture. God has given the church the Scriptures and the church has authority to infallibly announce condemnation and salvation.

Are Christians today any different than those religious leaders who challenged the authority of Jesus? Do they have contempt of authority? Yes, when they reject the authority of Scripture. The authority of Scripture must regulate what Christians think, believe, and practice. The following are a few examples I have heard through the years by professing Christians being challenged by the authority of God.

I know what the Bible says, but I believe. . . .

I know what the Bible says about how to worship God, but I believe....

I know what the Bible says about my responsibility to be salt and light to a lost world, but I believe....

> I know what the Bible says about my responsibility to witness the truth of gospel, but I believe....
>
> I know what the Bible says about restoring broken relationships, but I believe....

History is replete with those who say, "but I believe..."rather than "the Word of God is the final authority." The question of ultimate authority was troublesome for some of the people who were in the presence of the incarnate Jesus Christ, but it is also troublesome for some professing believers today. It is troublesome because some professing believers think in terms of the here and now. Known as proximate authority it is the authority Christians think they have now will eventually yield to the ultimate authority.

When the father sent his son to collect his profit from the tenants they rejected the son's authority, that is proximate authority (temporal authority), but the ultimate authority destroyed the tenants. (See Luke 20:9-18)

Contempt of rightly given proximate authority will result in justice by the ultimate authority.

Simply stated: If you reject the authority God has placed over you in this life, you will have contempt of authority when you stand before the ultimate authority.

The Danish philosopher, Soren Keirdegaard, once said, "I am not obliged to obey Paul because he is clever, or exceptionally clever, but I must submit to Paul because he has divine authority." (*The Zondervan Pictorial Encyclopedia of Bible*, "Authority," by H. D. McDonald, vol. 1, p. 421)

2. The Blessed Man

Blessed are the undefiled in the way, who walk in the law of the LORD! Blessed are those who keep His testimonies, Who seek Him with the whole heart! They also do no iniquity; They walk in His ways. You have commanded us to keep Your precepts diligently. Oh, that my ways were directed to keep Your statutes! Then I would not be ashamed, When I look into all Your commandments. I will praise You with uprightness of heart, When I learn Your righteous judgments. I will keep Your statutes Oh, do not forsake me utterly!

Psalm 119:1-8

Psalm 119 is one of the most extensive expressions of love for and obedience to the Word of God. The Psalmist refers to the Word of God by using seven terms synonymously and redundantly. They are:

God's Law
God's Word
God's Commandments
God's Statutes
God's Precepts
God's Testimonies
God's Judgments

The first stanza of this Psalm describes the way of the Lord which is obedience to the Word of God. There are two ways to travel in this life: the right way or the wrong way. The right way is God's way and the wrong way is man's way. The wisdom of Proverbs tells us that, "There is a way that seems right to a man, but its end is the way of death" (Proverbs 14:12). Obviously, man's way is the wrong way. Man's way is indeed a most dangerous way to travel. Man's way is most unpleasant and will eventually lead to death.

Although the Bible speaks generously about the way of the Lord, sometimes the Bible explains what happens when people ignore the way of the Lord. For instance, Amon the son of Manasseh forsook the Lord, the God of his fathers, and did not walk in the way of the Lord. Amon's own servants conspired against him and killed him in his own house (2 Kings 21:22). Contrary to man's way is God's way which is the right way. The way of the Lord has its effect. "The way of the Lord is a stronghold to the upright, but ruin to the workers of iniquity" (Proverbs 10:29).

The Bible clearly affirms that all people do not universally follow the way of the Lord. However, God's people love the way of the Lord. The reason is that the way of the Lord is the Word of God revealed in Holy Scripture; therefore Psalm 119 is for God's people, for it speaks to them alone.

When this Psalm was originally given, the only collected and written Word of God may very well have been the law of God, consisting primarily of the first five books of the Bible. However, there are other ways to express the law of the Lord such as His testimonies, His precepts or God's judgments.

The law given to Moses on Mt. Sinai is not merely a model for morality for God's people. The law did not just nationalize Israel. The law was not just a curse to those who disobey it. It is a binding covenant as any other of God's covenants with His people. Therefore, the law covenant is redemptive. Christians must remember that the law of God is the exact representation of Jesus Christ in His moral perfections. No doubt, the law of God is God's perfect moral standard for His people. However, the perpetual moral obligations in the law of God should not overshadow the covenantal blessings found in Christ the law keeper.

One thing is for certain. Whatever Scripture was available to the Psalmist at the time those words were inspired by God, was surely the center of his attention. He held the whole counsel of God close to his heart. The opening verses of this Psalm reveal the way of the Lord. Since the Word of God reveals the way of the Lord, the Word of God is the right way. The Word of God is to the soul what air is to the body. Without air the body will lose its life. Without the Word of God the soul will have no vitality.

The purity and sincerity of this Psalm describes the condition of the soul that knows, takes notice, and loves the Word of God. The condition of the soul is blessed when the Word of God is the basis for faith and obedience. To better understand the blessing, contrast a blessing with a curse. A curse is something bad and unwanted, so a blessing must be good and desirable.

Psalm one provides a contrast between a blessing and a curse. The blessed man loves the Word of God and meditates on it day and night. In contrast the wicked man or the cursed man is like a dead plant without roots. The blessed man has a firm foundation, but the ungodly are like chaff which the wind drives away. There is no end to the blessedness for the godly, but there is an end to wickedness. "The way of the ungodly shall perish" (Psalm 1:1-6). The ungodly will not perish for they have an eternal home, in an eternal inferno prepared for the Devil and his angels, but the way of the ungodly shall cease.

In contrast to the ungodly man is the blessed man. The blessed man has an eternal favorable relation with the true and living God. Blessedness describes the fellowship believers have with God because of His covenant promises.

Jesus describes the blessed man as Jesus gave His discourse commonly called the sermon of the mount (Mathew 5:3-12). Some translations substitute the word "happy" for the word blessed. That is a half-poor translation. The word "blessed" in Matthew as in the text in Psalm 119 means more than mere happiness as many people understand the English word "happiness". Blessedness comes from God's grace. It means there is divine favor. The word "happy" more often than not carries with it the idea that one is delighted or pleased about something or someone.

The word "happy" is characterized by pleasure and good fortune. Relative to the Christian world and life view, it may not be the best choice when clarity is important. You should understand what a word means if you use it. The word "happy" has its origin not in some ancient language, but in the Old English word "hap." The word "hap" referred to luck, chance, or fortune. I'm sure you've heard the old expression "happy-go-lucky person." He is the carefree unconcerned let luck come my way person. Such is the way of life of the happy-go-lucky man and it is the way of an ungodly world and life view.

Robert Ingersoll, one of the leading liberals of the 19th century once said, "happiness is the only good." If you search literature you will find that the word "happiness" was not used nearly as much until after the French Revolution by philosophers and theologians.

The word that preceded "happiness" in every day use was the word "good," particularly in theological discourse. There was a time when Christians emphasized goodness over happiness. Happiness is associated with human experience, but the word "good" is associated with praising the excellency of something or someone. Happiness is subjective. Goodness is objective. Rather than using the word happy, I prefer words like contentment, joy, and peace because they describe a condition that reflects the blessedness that comes from the grace of God. Philosophical inquiry may make a man happy, but it will not bring contentment. Social improvement may make a man happy, but it will not bring joy. Religious activity may make a man happy, but it will not bring peace. What is it that will assure Christians of contentment, joy, and peace? The answer is the blessed man.

The Psalmist has wonderfully integrated the good man's condition, which is morally measured by the Word of God, with the man who experiences contentment, joy, and peace. If you want to have a right relationship with God, then there must be moral legislation that you personally love.

All moral legislation which comes from the Word of God will bring contentment, joy and peace in your life. The blessed man shows his blessedness by being blameless in his way. Blameless does not mean sinless perfection, but it does mean Christians have a perfect rule to follow in the Word of God. It is the ultimate authority for the soul.

The blessed man shows his blessedness by walking in the law of the Lord. It is in the Word of God that Christians find the mind of God. It is in the Word of God that Christians are instructed to walk in the way of the Lord. You will find the Lord's way in the Lord's Word. The blessed man shows his blessedness by seeking the Lord with his whole heart. If you want to know God's will for your life, you will find it in the Word of God. The blessing that comes from the Word of God cannot be fully comprehended. I am yet to understand why professing Christians do not love the Word to the point of making it a priority in life. "Then I would not be ashamed, when I look into all Your commandments" (Psalm 119:6).

The Psalmist declares that his shame was removed by looking at the Word of God? His looking was not just a glance; it was a serious study and deep meditation that removed his shame. The Psalmist saw the holy nature and character of God, the sinfulness of man and the way of God's redemption.

The prayer of the Psalmist ought to be the prayer of every Christian: "do not forsake me utterly" (Psalm 119:8)! The child of God ought to have assurance that God will not utterly abandon His elect. There may be times when God does not appear to have His favorable hand upon His people, but God will never desert His elect.

The prayer is in the context of the pilgrim Christian seeking God's way from the Word of God. Study God's Word and you will learn God's way. Lay it up in your heart. Meditate upon the Word of God.

3. Ultimate Authority for Young People

How can a young man cleanse his way; By taking heed according to Your Word. With my whole heart I have sought You; Oh, let me not wander from Your commandments! Your Word I have hidden in my heart, that I might not sin against You. Blessed are You, O LORD! Teach me Your statutes. With my lips I have declared All the judgments of Your mouth. I have rejoiced in the way of Your testimonies, As much as in all riches. I will meditate on Your precepts, And contemplate Your ways. I will delight myself in Your statutes; I will not forget Your Word.

Psalm 119:9-16

The young man must understand the ultimate authority for the soul. The words "young man" derive from the Hebrew Word *naar* which is also translated children (Job 29, Psalm 148). It is in the masculine form, but that does not restrict it from applying to young men and women. In the Hebrew culture the male was said to represent the females. Patriarchialism was a common practice. However, females are not excluded from accountability to the Word of God.

The Psalmist begins with a question and answer about a young man in his minority and his relationship with the Word of God. In the remainder of the verses the Psalmist speaking in the first person reflects on his life and his relationship with the Word of God as a man of majority and maturity. There is a question that should be on the hearts and tongues of people all over this country. "How can a young man cleanse his way?" How many young people are asking that question? Some young people may ask the question, "What can I do with my life today that will make me rich and famous?" Others may ask the question, "How can I survive in this miserable world?"

I was in high school in the late 1950s and early 60s. The hard core group in my school smoked cigarettes, but not in front of adults, they had an occasional alcoholic beverage, and occasionally somebody may commit a notorious crime and steal a watermelon.

Each generation since that time has increased the mischief to the point that now taking human life is the ultimate thrill. However, murder has been an acceptable way of life for every generation since the Fall in the Garden of Eden. Cain murdered his own brother. Sin is a curse to the human race. Sin affected the race, "And even as they did not like to retain God in their knowledge, God gave them over to a debased mind, to do things which are not fitting" (Romans 1:28). The question remains, "how can a young man cleanse his way?"

The Bible explains, with ultimate authority, the way to have peace with God and experience a new direction in life. "Therefore having been justified by faith, we have peace with God through our Lord Jesus Christ" (Romans 5:1). The only way a young man can cleanse his way is by belonging to Jesus Christ. The apostle Paul explains how to belong to Christ. "Believe on the Lord Jesus Christ" (Acts 16:31).

Unfortunately, many young people receive a distorted view of authority from a biblical perspective. They have not been taught the relationship of God's law to the authority of Scripture. God's law is universal in its scope.

> For when Gentiles who do not have the law by nature do the things in the law, these, although not have the law, are a law to themselves, who show the work of the law written in their hearts, their conscience also bearing witness. (Romans 2:14-15).

The rejection of natural law and biblical authority is one of the many reasons for the total disregard for life among many young people. The prevailing power of sin does not totally and forever squeeze out the law of God. Unbelievers know better, but because of their sinful nature they suppress the knowledge of God's law, reject His ultimate authority and act wickedly.

The Psalmist posed a rhetorical question: "How can a young man cleanse his way?" His question was addressed to the covenant community in Israel, now referred to as the Christian community. Unbelievers are unable to answer the question because they have a corrupt view of biblical authority and God's law.

The child of God asserts that a young man can cleanse his way, "By taking heed according to Your Word" (Psalm 119:9). Christian young people will find a wealth of perfect principles in the Word of God. The Bible instructs and commands Christians to "let the Word of Christ dwell richly in you" (Colossians 3:16). Christians are to bring every thought captive to the obedience of Jesus Christ (2 Corinthians 10:5). The Christian world and life view is the standard philosophy of life for instructing young people. Only those who belong to Jesus Christ can love God's authority and obey His law.

Professing Christians make comments like "our country must turn back to God." Our country was never turned to God in the first place. I take it that "our country" refers to the establishment of the Articles of Confederation adopted by congress on November 15, 1777. Until that time "our country" remained a servant to King George the tyrant. It was from those early years when the puritans and pilgrims settled this country until the War for Independence that the colonies were under the influence of Puritan clergy, Puritan businessmen, and Puritan political leaders. They were a formidable force and they enforced the law of God. After the establishment of "our country" the law of God became less and less important in the public sector. Respect for authority has been reduced to victimizationalism. I believe that the Christian influence virtually ended in 1954 when the Supreme Court ruled against the Sabbath principle for our society. Professing Christians ought to say, "the church must turn back to God."

Young people and old people must turn to the Bible for the answer to the moral dilemma. The Bible emphasizes the importance of teaching young people the Word of God. "And these Words which I command you today shall be in your heart. You shall teach them diligently to your children, and shall talk of them when you sit in your house, when you walk by the way, when you lie down, and when you rise up" (Deuteronomy 6:6-7).

Parents have the responsibility to teach their children a Christian world and life view and parents have the Word of God to teach them. A Christian world and life view will teach young people why they must preserve life and property and how they can be instruments of saving life and property.

It is not enough to hand a young person a Bible and charge them with the responsibility to read, understand, and apply it. The lives of young people are in a state of change. They are changing from a child to an adult. Hormonal changes will cause affections to rise. They sense the rapid change and they possess vast amounts of energy. What they do not possess is wisdom and understanding. A Christian world and life view will show young people how to use their energy to develop the wisdom and understanding they do not possess in their youth.

Although the Psalmist draws attention to a man in his youth with a rhetorical question and answer, he also reveals his testimony as a man of maturity. Looking back over his life he could say: "With my whole heart I have sought after God." The Psalmist did not mean he was seeking God with a perfect heart, but with all his power and ability.

The Word of God belongs in the soul. To use the metaphor, "Your Word I have hidden in my heart" is a reference to the authority of the Word of God in the soul of man. Hide the Word of God with all its doctrines, precepts, promises, threats, and examples so that in times of danger and oppression you can call upon it for relief and comfort. The Word of God belongs to the soul for eternal purposes.

There is a story, I presume to be true, of a Roman Catholic Priest who took a Bible from a young man and burned it. The young man said, "You cannot burn the Word of God which I have in my heart." The Psalmist expresses his passion for the Word of God in Psalm 119:9-16:

> Taking heed according to Your Word
> Let me not wander from Your commandments
> Your Word I have hidden in my heart
> Teach me Your statutes
> I have declared all the judgments of Your mouth
> I have rejoiced in the way of Your testimonies
> I will meditate on Your precepts
> I will not forget Your Word

Having the Word of God in his soul from his youth, his decisions in life were based on the truth of the Word of God. The greatest pursuit in this life is God Himself. The greatest peril in this life is wandering away from God.

When the desires of this earthly life clash with the will of God and when the temptations of power and pleasure overwhelm you, take heed to the Word of God. Rejoice in the Word of God, meditate upon it, find your delight in the Word of God and never, never, forget it. The Word of God is the ultimate authority for your soul.

4. Open My Eyes

Deal bountifully with Your servant, That I may live and keep Your Word. Open my eyes, that I may see wondrous things from Your law. I am a stranger in the earth; Do not hide Your commandments from me. My soul breaks with longing for Your judgments at all times. You rebuke the proud—the cursed, Who stray from Your commandments. Remove from me reproach and contempt, for I have kept Your testimonies. Princes also sit and speak against me, but Your servant meditates on Your statutes. Your testimonies also are my delight and my counselors.

Psalm 119:17-24

The first thought that comes to mind from this portion of Psalm 119 is the relationship between the Psalmist and God. The Psalmist calls himself a servant of God. It would be unthinkable to apply the Word of God in Psalm 119 to an unbeliever. Believing the Word of God and having a passion to live by the Word of God is evidence of being in a right relationship with God. This is very important because the Word of God has mysterious doctrine that is unbelievable without the Spirit of God revealing the truth in the Word of God.

The believer in this Psalm goes to God with a command of entreaty and prays that God will deal bountifully with the believer. To deal bountifully means to bring to maturity. For instance a mother nurses a child, but she eventually weans the child when it becomes mature enough to eat on its own. A fruit begins as a flower and turns into a fruit. When the fruit is fully ripe it will fall into your hand. This is the notion in the mind of the Psalmist and should be your notion that God will bring you to full maturity. Unfortunately, some Christians do not mature, but act like "mere men" (1 Corinthians 3:1-4).

The Psalmist wants to come to full maturity and he gives two reasons. He wants to live and keep the Word of God. Ponder the words of the Psalmist because they should be the words of every Christian. This is a prayer for believers. They are just as applicable to you today as they were the day they were written. This prayer has two parts. The first part of the prayer is, "Bring me to full maturity O Lord that I may live." The second part of the prayer is, "Bring me to full maturity O Lord that I may keep the Word of God."

People have the desire to live. Their motivations are several. No one has ever figured out why some people have a desire to live more than others. For the sake of time and brevity, life may be described as the universal condition of the human race continuing in this present world.

We contrast life to death. It is universally assumed that death is the termination of the human being in this present world. All grant that death takes the human being beyond the realm of this world. It is often said that life is precious. Some qualification must be made, because life is precious to some and an eternal liability to others.

The unbeliever rebels against the Creator and the Bible explains it would be best if the unbeliever was never born. In fact he or she should not consider life as precious because the end of life brings eternal condemnation. In fact, the shorter the life of the unbeliever, the fewer his sins will be and the final judgment will be less severe. So for the unbeliever life is a liability.

If Christians had a compassionate bone in their body they should busy themselves with defending the true religion and devoting themselves to the spread of the gospel so that the unbeliever might believe and live. Jesus said to his disciples, "I came that they [my sheep] may have life and, and that they have it more abundantly" (John 10:10). It must be stressed that this Psalm is not for the unbeliever and those words of Jesus were not directed to the unbeliever. The Psalmist wrote this inspired prayer for the believer. Jesus wanted to assure the believer that Satan's lies brought death, but Jesus brought life.

The Christian is greatly blessed to have life. An elect man or woman should desire the bountiful long life. The reason is that the Christian goes from election to glorification by way of sanctification. If God gives a good long life it gives the Christian plenty of time to exercise his gifts and abilities to the glory of God.

Christians "keep the Word of God" to glorify God with their gifts and abilities. The Word of God tells us what to do to glorify God. The interminable problem many Christians face is that they do not know what to do to glorify God. Your own ideas will not glorify God. Your own private agenda will not glorify God. You cannot do anything to please God unless He tells you how to please Him. This is an eternal biblical principle taught throughout Scripture; it is also a matter of common sense. You cannot satisfy God in any way, shape, fashion, or form unless you know what God wants.

The only place you will find out what God expects is from His own mouth. The mouth of God is the Word of God. Simply reading the Word of God is not sufficient. It is for that reason that the Psalmist prayed to the Lord "open my eyes." The Bible tells the story of the blind man crying out to Jesus, "Son of David have mercy on me." Then Jesus responded, "What do you want me to do for you?" And the blind man said to Him, "My master, I want to regain my sight." (See Mark 10:46-52.)

If someone considers physical sight valuable, how much more valuable is spiritual sight. The Psalmist certainly has spiritual eyesight in mind. The Word of God is spiritual and clearly the Word of God is the goal for the Psalmist. The value of spiritual sight has glorious eternal consequences.

A question that arises from this text is, "Why would a believer pray for the opening of his eyes? The spiritual eyes of God's children are opened by degrees. The Psalmist had some understanding of the Word of God, but he wanted more. He wanted to be enlightened by the Word of God. As much as he desired a clearer and fuller understanding of the Word of God, he did not ask for new revelation. The Word of God written was sufficient for him. Every Christian should be satisfied with the full counsel of God. I cannot understand why anyone would want more revelation from God when the Bible is virtually untouched by most Christians. What the Psalmist prays for is what we should be praying for and that is illumination from God. Pray that God would illumine our minds by the mighty working of His Holy Spirit to receive and understand his Word. God gives the believer "the spirit of wisdom and revelation in the knowledge of Christ" (Ephesians 1:17), so that the eyes of man's understanding may be enlightened.

The unbeliever on the other hand lives in darkness in relation to God's Word, "the eyes of their understanding being darkened, being alienated from the life of God" (Ephesians 4:18). Wicked natural men do not find any wonder in the Word of God because the Word of God has the eternal nature and character of God in sight, which unbelievers despise. The unbeliever cannot see the beauty of God's law and God's love, neither of which can be known without understanding the Word of God.

God gives Christians the same spirit He gave Moses and the apostle Paul. Since they cannot go to Moses or Paul and ask them to explain the Word of God or ask them the meaning of the Word, they have the Spirit of God to open their eyes that Christians may behold wondrous things from the Word of God. The word "wondrous" refers to the extraordinary.

The Psalmist used personal relative language so every Christian may see the Word of God for himself or herself. For example, the Psalmist emphasized, "that I may live" and "that I may behold." That personal relative language continues throughout the Psalm as the Psalmist prays for understanding.

The Psalmist makes an observation that every Christian should carefully consider. The Psalmist said, "I am a stranger in the earth." The Christian is merely a sojourner traveling through this world to reach the eternal home. Man's greatest care should be for that place where he lives the longest. The Christian is a stranger to this world and should set his or her sights not upon the things of this world, but upon the things of the world to come. The writer of Hebrews explains the kind of place the Christian seeks. In Hebrews 11:10 the man of God is, "looking for the city which has foundations whose architect and builder is God." Although Christians are pilgrims, they have the blessing of God in this life, but only as that blessedness is revealed in the Word of God. The Bible explains how to shape your life by the ultimate authority for the soul.

The Word of God makes Christians wise unto salvation. The Word of God is the only way they may be properly prepared for the eternal kingdom to come. The passion of the Psalmist was not money, fame, property, family, church, or any earthly institution. His passion was an intense earnest desire for the Word of God. This man wanted to be filled with the Word of God.

The Psalmist was not the only one who felt that way. The apostle Paul said the same thing in different words to the Corinthian Church. Paul said to take every thought captive to the obedience of Christ (2 Corinthians 10:5). Every thought, whether that thought is fleeting or ponderous, it should be subject to the Word of God.

It is for that reason that the Psalmist could say, "I long for your Word at all times." Whether in adversity or in plenty, Christians should find comfort and hope in the Word of God. The proud man has no use for the Word of God. It is to him an obstacle to his self-aggrandizement. The proud man elevates himself in this world and ignores the Word of God for his own ego.

The believer on the other hand prays that God will remove any reproach or contempt. The believer listens carefully to the Word of God, which is nothing less than the voice of God. The man of God who loves the Word of God will be the object of scorn by the unbeliever. The Psalmist explains how unbelievers will "sit and talk against me." However, God's children will meditate upon and seek counsel from the Word of God. They will say "my delight" is God's Word.

The Word of God reveals the truth of God's saving grace. It reveals the mercy of God in Jesus Christ. The Word of God reveals God's wisdom for living life.

5. Understand God's Truth

My soul clings to the dust; Revive me according to Your Word. I have declared my ways, and You answered me; Teach me Your statutes. Make me understand the way of Your precepts; So shall I meditate on Your wonderful works. My soul melts from heaviness; Strengthen me according to Your Word. Remove from me the way of lying, and grant me Your law graciously. I have chosen the way of truth; Your judgments I have laid before me. I cling to Your testimonies; O LORD, do not put me to shame! I will run the course of Your commandments, for You shall enlarge my heart.

Psalm 119:25-32

This Psalm is specifically for and applies to the child of God. If you love Jesus Christ and want to obey Him you will love this Psalm. It is a Psalm that speaks to the very heart of the Christian soul. This Psalm reveals the absolute supremacy of God's sovereign hand.

The Psalmist must have experienced terrible circumstances and described the situation as, "My soul cleaves to the dust." He speaks as if he is glued to this earth and properly the word "dust" refers to earthly things. The earth and all rational beings are part of a depraved creation. This kind of language is present throughout the Bible. It describes the child of God as a stranger or a pilgrim on this earth. The Psalmist responds to this dilemma proactively by declaring, "I cling to Your testimonies." He was at one time glued to the things of this world, but now he is glued to the Word of God. A Christian may make a concentrated effort to learn the Ten Commandments, but knowing them is not enough. Professing Christians ought to ask God to enable them to understand the Ten Commandments. Knowledge and understanding depends on the spiritual condition of the soul. The soul of a child of God not only has knowledge, he or she will have understanding. However, children of God are susceptible to the dangers of misunderstanding the ultimate authority for the soul. The apostle Peter said, "our beloved brother Paul, according to the wisdom given to him, has written to you, as also in all his epistles, speaking in them of these things, in which are some things hard to understand, which untaught and unstable people twist to their own destruction, as they do also the rest of the Scriptures" (2 Peter 3:15-16).

Christians ought not judge the salvation of anyone, but remember the deadly influence of sin according to their own standard and measure. The only possible way to see the import, influence, and impact of sin in our lives is from the Word of God. The pilgrim Christians should ascend to the excellency of God's Word where they find instructions for relief from the sinfulness of this world. The Word of God does not operate mysteriously to remove the sin from your life, nor does the Word of God remove the sin that surrounds you. The Word of God will make you understand the operation of sin, the influence of sin, and the extent of sin in this present world.

The Psalmist realized, as Christians should, that the Word of God is the ultimate authority for the soul. I cringe when Christians say, "My heart leads me and strengthens me." This is what the Bible says about that subject. "The heart is deceitful above all things and desperately wicked" (Jeremiah 17:9). Sometimes that wickedness is a perverted form of wickedness found in the church.

> For among My people are found wicked men; They lie in wait as one who sets snares; They set a trap; They catch men. As a cage is full of birds, so their houses are full of deceit. Therefore they have become great and grown rich. (Jeremiah 5:26-27)

Jeremiah preached during the time that Jerusalem was under siege by the Babylonians. The Israelite culture was in chaos. The leaders in Jerusalem tried to soothe over the problem by saying, "Peace, peace." However, the religious community (Old Testament Church) was "full of deceit." The contemporary church is no different. They have become great and grown rich, but they are full of deceit. The truth of that assertion is self-evident. They have refused to come under the ultimate authority for the soul.

If the heart is deceitful and wicked men are among us (the church), I find, with no little surprise, that our strength is directly related to truth. Among the sins that could have been mentioned, lies and deception is in the forefront. In stark contrast is the truth in the Word of God. Obviously, the Psalmist has the ninth commandment in mind. "Thou shall not bear false witness against your neighbor." The ninth commandment is primarily concerned with communicating truth. The Bible teaches that the church is the pillar and foundation of truth and that truth transcends time and cultures. The Psalmist put it in these terms: "For His lovingkindness is great toward us, and the truth of the Lord is everlasting" (Psalm 117:2).

At the time the ninth commandment was given to Moses, the terminology, "to bear false witness" referred to the legal process used in Israel in which a person was expected to give a response at a trial. A truthful response described that which really happened. When you are on the witness stand, you are required to tell the truth about your neighbor. When we apply the principle in the 9th commandment to ourselves, we are all on trial, God is the judge and truth will prevail.

The way to measure truth is to understand the nature of God. The Psalmist said, "The sum of Thy Word is truth" (Psalm 119.160). The ultimate standard for truth is the mind of God, therefore the ultimate authority for the soul of man is the Word of God. Since truth is so important to the soul of man and God's Word is the ultimate authority for the soul, it is the duty of the Christian to study God's Word and pray for understanding and discernment.

Doctrinal indifference is eating away at the once strong church in North America, because some local particular churches are starved for truth. The way we treat people reflects the depth of understanding that we have of truth or the lack of understanding truth in its relationship to God's moral law. Whether against God, our neighbor or ourselves, we learn from John chapter eight that where there is a lie on the tongue, Satan is in the heart.

The ninth commandment teaches that a lie is a lie. It has been argued that a lie in the interest of a greater good is not really a lie. The Bible does not speak of any circumstances that directly or implies a person may tell a lie and be commended by God. A lie is always a sin. If lying has prevailed in your life, there is refuge in the righteousness of the one who is the Truth, the Lord Jesus Christ.

The pilgrim life is not easy. The obstacles and challenges make the journey of life complex and sometimes the body struggles because leaders abuse the law of authority. The authority structure for life on earth is given by injunction in the fifth commandment, (honor your father and mother). However, the principle is further explained in Scripture to extend to pastors, teachers, employers, political leaders and others in the place of authority. If truth and authority trouble you, get out of the dust and cling to the Word of God. Stay glued to the authority that will never disappoint the soul. Say, "I will run the course of Your commandments, for You shall enlarge my heart" (Psalm 119:32).

This chapter may be summarized from two perspectives, one negative and one positive. The negative perspective is, do not look for your heart to direct you through life. The positive perspective is look to the Word of God to direct you through life, because it is your ultimate authority for the soul. Pray that the Holy Spirit will convict you so the Word of God may convince you.

6. Spiritual Discernment

Teach me, O Lord, the way of Your statutes, and I shall keep it to the end. Give me understanding, and I shall keep Your law; Indeed, I shall observe it with my whole heart. Make me walk in the path of Your commandments, for I delight in it. Incline my heart to Your testimonies, and not to covetousness. Turn away my eyes from looking at worthless things, and revive me in Your way. Establish Your Word to Your servant, who is devoted to fearing You. Turn away my reproach which I dread, for Your judgments are good. Behold, I long for Your precepts; Revive me in Your righteousness.

Psalm 119:33-40

God's commandments are also called injunctions. For instance God told Abraham, "take now your son" that was a commandment. Hebrew grammarians refer to it as the imperative mood. These verses in Psalm 119 sound like commandments from the Psalmist, commanding the Lord.

It is beyond the scope of the Christian mind to think that God could be ordered to do something, so these imperatives are petitions. It is pleading to the Lord with a request, even though it may sound like a command. Sometimes these are referred to as imperatives of entreaty. The Psalmist makes an appeal to the Lord with forceful language as possible. These appeals, requests, or petitions literally describe the Psalmist begging the Lord to act on behalf of the Psalmist. The Psalmist has eight petitions offered as a prayer to the Lord.

One of the petitions is, "Teach me thy statutes." The New International Version translates it, "Teach me, O Lord, to follow your decrees." The words statute and decree are not commonly used in our everyday language. For the sake of definition we understand that the word "statute" is most often associated with a rule or regulation officially established by some governing body.

The term "statutory law" is the expressed will of a legislative body in written form which is to be distinguished from some unwritten or common law.

In the context of this Psalm the word "statutes" refers to God's law, His written law, specifically His written moral law. In connection with God's moral law the Psalmist begs God to teach him. When we put his prayer in the context of the whole verse we find the Psalmist begging the Lord for instruction in the law of God. Every Christian should be willing to pray like the Psalmist.

> Teach me, O Lord, the way of Your statutes.
> Give me understanding.
> Make me walk in the path of Your commandments.

Notice the ascending order of these prayerful petitions. If Christians go to the Lord in prayer and say, "teach me" they must have the rational capacity to be taught. The next level in this prayer is, "give me understanding." Discernment is the ability to distinguish between the true and the false. The apostle Paul explains discernment from a biblical perspective. "But the natural man does not receive the things of the Spirit of God, for they are foolishness to him; nor can he know them, because they are spiritually discerned" (1 Corinthians 2:14; also see John 8:43-47).

There are about 700,000 English words (circa) in the Bible; every word comes from the mouth of God, therefore every word in the Bible is important. Since God's store of knowledge is so vast, Christians must pray for understanding.

Once you have been taught the raw data, and given the ability to sort it out and you can make sense out of it, then the next step is a galactic challenge. Would you be willing to ask God to make you walk in the way of His commandments?

Knowing the doctrine of Scripture is prerequisite to living according the Word of God. "Make me walk in the path of Your commandments" is the request of the Psalmist. However, many professing Christians talk in terms of, "but, theology." I mentioned this in chapter one; however, it is important enough to repeat it.

> I know what the Bible teaches, but...
> I know what the Bible says about worship, but...
> I know the Bible teaches predestination, but...
> I know the Bible teaches truth, but...
> I know the Bible teaches God is sovereign, but...

This outline could continue with "I know, but" and this is one of the most popular theological disasters among professing Christians. "I know what the Bible teaches, but" attempts to rob God of His ultimate authority.

This prayer further calls God to, "Incline my heart to Your testimonies" (Psalm 119:36). The "heart" in this context must be a reference to the "will." A child of God needs his or her will changed to enable him or her to be taught, understand, and walk according to the Word of God. The word "testimonies" is a synonym for commandments and commandments is a synonym for God's law, statutes, and testimonies, therefore commandments in this context refers to the whole counsel of God.

The Psalmist needed a change of heart, specifically that aspect of his heart called the will, so he might be enabled to act upon what he had been taught to discern from the Word of God. Human beings are naturally obstinate and have the desire to disobey God rather than obey God. To obey the Lord in a general sense is practically impossible so the Psalmist becomes very specific: He wants to be inclined to obey God and turn away from covetousness. For some reason, the Psalmist chooses covetousness over the other commandments of God as the object of his obedience. However, there is a sense in which all sins can be traced to three root sins. They are pride, lust, and covetousness. Actually they can't be completely separated, but covetousness is the queen of all sins. Adam and Eve could not resist the temptation and the sin of covetousness was irresistible. "So when the woman saw that the tree was good for food, that it was pleasant to the eyes, and a tree desirable to make one wise, she took of its fruit and ate. She also gave to her husband with her, and he ate" (Genesis 3:6). The Hebrew word translated "covet" or "desire" carries with it the idea of a passionate pleasure. Not necessarily just sexual lust or any unfulfilled appetite of some sort, but any inordinate desire to have something that God has chosen not to supply at a particular time.

The sin of coveting is closely associated with the sinful human will. If the will has not been renewed by the power of the Holy Spirit it is a self-seeking will (See 2 Timothy 3:2ff). An inordinate love for self is the mark of fallen man. Therefore, covetousness is in competition with God's ultimate authority. Covetousness intermingles with other commandments. Covetousness works with murder. For instance, someone wants the reputation of another man, but they cannot gain it so they slander him/her to raise their own ego.

Covetousness often accompanies sexual lust. When a person can't have certain material things, they steal because the heart covets the things of this world. Telling lies and covetousness often go together. For instance, someone is not willing to think intelligently, so he/she tells lies to try and impress people, because he/she covets attention. Covetousness is related to the other commandments because covetousness is an inward problem. The Bible Affirms this universal principle; "Each one is tempted when he is drawn away by his own desires" (James 1:14). The inspired writers of Holy Scripture associated covetousness with the most evil practices known to men. The Psalmist said, "The wicked boasts of his heart's desire and the greedy man curses and spurns the Lord" (Psalm 10:3).

Covetousness is not only a heart sin that leads to sinful human relationships, but covetousness has the potential to drive a wedge between man and God as it did in the garden of Eden. The covetous man (generic for men and women) curses and spurns the Lord. The covetous man is not content with God's promises, so he turns his back on God, which is the same as cursing and spurning. The covetous man does what is right in his own eyes. The covetous man takes great pain to gain the things of this world and cares little, if any, about eternal life and the heavenly home. The covetous man spends his time talking about this world. The covetous man is more interested in the business world, the sports world, the recreation world, and in short his/her own world than the world to come. The covetous man will not have an appetite for spiritual things. The preaching of the Word of God and the sacraments do not appeal to him, because they speak to the soul, not the body.

The covetous soul turns away from ultimate authority. It was for that reason the Psalmist said, "turn away my eyes from looking at worthless things" (Psalm 119:37). Worthless things translated in the King James Version refers to vanity, useless-ness, that which is false, or not of real importance. Vanity refers to worldly pleasure, worldly honor, worldly profit – all of which implies worldly happiness. The vain things of this world deceive with the promise of earthly happiness.

Your heart's desire for autonomous authority finds its source in a sinful covetous soul or your heart's desire is the authority of God from His Word. Christians must pray pas-sionately:

Teach me, O Lord.
Give me understanding.

Make me walk in Your ways.
Turn away my eyes for looking at worthless things.
Establish Your Word to Your servant,
Who is devoted to fearing You.

Revive me in Your righteousness.

7. Mercy With Truth

Let Your mercies come also to me, O Lord—Your salvation according to Your Word. So shall I have an answer for him who reproaches me, for I trust in Your Word. And take not the Word of truth utterly out of my mouth, for I have hoped in Your ordinances. So shall I keep Your law continually, forever and ever. And I will walk at liberty, for I seek Your precepts. I will speak of Your testimonies also before kings, and will not be ashamed. And I will delight myself in Your commandments, which I love. My hands also I will lift up to Your commandments, which I love, and I will meditate on Your statutes.

Psalm 119:41-48

The way of the Lord is full of mercy with truth. Since the way of the Lord is contrary to the way of a sinful heart, Christians must have the Word of God to show them the Lord's way. The way of the Lord according to His Word is the prevailing theme throughout Psalm 119. The Psalmist repeats the theme over and over. For instance, Psalm 119:9 calls attention to the young man and the proverbial question, "How can a young man cleanse his way?" The Psalmist answers that rhetorical question; "By taking heed according to Your Word." The Word of God is the means by which Christian parents should shape the minds of the young people, so that they develop a godly world and life view.

Christians should think carefully before they blame the world on the culture wars produced by modernity or the re-defining notion of the postmodern world. It is the absence of the Christian world and life view that plagues the church. For several generations the church has not given young people a Christian world and life view and now those who were young people have produced this present culture. It is alleged that the greatest enemy of the Word of God is the modern world (secularism and its ally, the scientific method). Some claim the greatest enemy of the Word of God is the postmodern culture. The Word of God is not in competition with conceptual demonstrations of the scientific community or the postmodern influences. The Word of God is the rule of faith and life. It is the basis and foundation for the Christian belief system. It is the standard for life and the way Christians live.

Unfortunately life begins with an unfavorable relationship with God (Psalm 51:5; 58:3). The only hope to restore a favorable relationship is for God to grant grace and mercy. God's saving grace is the fruit of His mercy applied to His people according to His Word. The way of salvation is revealed in the Word of God and applied effectually by the power of the Holy Spirit. The Psalmist said, "Let Your mercies come also to me, O Lord—Your salvation according to Your Word" (Psalm 119:41). The New International Version and the Revised Standard Version translate it "according to your promise." God's Word is replete with God's promises.

The saving act is an act of God. Salvation is described in the Word of God and salvation is promised in the Word of God. Whether by description or promise, salvation is from God. Paul, the inspired apostle, uses a series of rhetorical questions in his letter to the Romans to explain that the salvation of God's people is uniquely related to the Word of God.

> How then shall they call on Him in whom they have not believed? And how shall they believe in Him of whom they have not heard? And how shall they hear without a preacher? And how shall they preach unless they are sent? As it is written: How beautiful are the feet of those who preach the gospel of peace, who bring glad tiding of good things. (Romans 10:14)

Salvation is not magic. Salvation is sensible and understandable to the renewed mind. The Psalmist understood and so should Christians that salvation is from God according to God's Word.

In the context of this prayer it is obvious that the Psalmist fears some danger or feels threatened. That makes perfectly good sense because Christians cannot think of salvation without thinking of danger. When they think of eternal salvation, they cannot help but think of the opposite which is eternal condemnation. However, it appears that the Psalmist has temporal salvation in mind more than eternal salvation.

Whether we are saved from a tornado or saved from eternal damnation, our trust is ultimately in God as He reveals His justice and mercy in His Word. The only way a sinner can be saved is for God to execute His justice. Of course we understand that God's justice falls upon the Lord Jesus Christ instead of the sinner who deserves God's justice. Do we deserve salvation? No, we deserve justice. We deserve to be punished according to the crimes we have committed. Do we want justice? No, we want mercy. The sinner's prayer is the same prayer of the Psalmist; "Let your mercies come also to me, O Lord." The Psalmist did not ask the Lord for mercy – as a general conceptual rule. The Psalmist said "mercies" (plural). Jeremiah's response to God's mercies is joyfully glorious.

> Through the Lord's mercies we are not consumed, because His compassions fail not. They are new every morning; Great is your faithfulness. "The Lord is my portion," says my soul, "therefore I hope in Him." (Lamentations 3:22-24)

God's promise from the inspired and infallible Word, spoken from the mouth of the prophet Hosea and the Psalmist is the same. God's position is clear. "For I desire mercy, not sacrifice, and the knowledge of God rather than burnt offerings" (Hosea 6:6). The word "mercy" comes from the Hebrew word *chesed* which is translated lovingkindness 176 times in the Old Testament. Mercy is relative to lovingkindness. The Bible teaches that the, "Lord is longsuffering and abundant in mercy [lovingkindness]" (Numbers 14:18) and that the, "earth is full of the mercy [lovingkindness] of the Lord" (Psalm 33:5). The mercy of God is at the forefront of your existence. Just stop and think for one minute how much mercy God demonstrates to a sinner such as you. Mercy reflects love which, can be summarized from God's Word. "First you shall love the Lord your God. Second, you shall love your neighbor" (*Return to the Lord*, by Martin Murphy, p. 61).

The prophet Micah elaborates on the doctrine of mercy relative to God's expectation. "And what does the Lord require of you? To act justly and to love mercy and walk humbly with your God" (Micah 6:8). Love mercy requires acts of kindness by forgiving and reconciliation when relationships fall apart.

Christians need God's mercy and salvation so they will have an answer for unbelievers who find fault with the believer's faith and trust in God. The Psalmist, like all Christians, desires and prays for mercy because they are ridiculed for their faith and trust in God's Word.

When Christians are abused, they must appeal to the ultimate authority. The most desirable relief for God's people will be found in the Word of truth. "And take not the Word of truth utterly out of my mouth, for I have hoped in Your ordinances" (Psalm 119:43). Truth was certainly desirable to the mind of the Psalmist. The Psalmist not only wanted to know the truth, he wanted to speak the truth.

If there is no absolute truth, there is no absolute authority. Some evangelicals associate truth almost exclusively to ethics and morality. To put it another way they seem to think that truth exists to define our ethical norms and moral practices.

Moral judgments certainly depend on ultimate truth, but truth is an attribute of God. Truth is a testimony of God's rational, reasonable, and logical character. Pilate's question is the right question. "What is truth?" The answer is, "God is truth." Since God is truth and He demands truthfulness from His children the place to discover truth is from the Word of God. Although truth is the fundamental characteristic of God's Word, it is specifically used in the book of Psalms 33 times. The following verses have something to say about truth.

> Psalm 51:6 - "Surely you desire truth in the inner parts; you teach me wisdom in the inmost place." The inner parts refer to the depth of your being, your soul.

> Psalm 69:13 - "But as for me, my prayer is to Thee, O Lord, at an acceptable time; O God, in the greatness of Thy lovingkindness answer me with Thy saving truth." There is no salvation without truth.

> Psalm 85:11 - "Truth springs from the earth; And righteousness looks down from heaven." The Psalmist used Hebrew parallelism to show the extent of truth, heaven, and earth.

> Psalm 86:11 - "Teach me Thy way, O Lord; I will walk in Thy truth; Unite my heart to fear Thy name." Christians must not only believe truth, they must practice truth.

> Psalm 117:2 - "For His lovingkindness is great toward us, and the truth of the Lord is everlasting." Truth will never end.

> Psalm 119:142 - "Thy righteousness is an everlasting righteousness, and Thy law is truth."

> Psalm 119:151- "Thou art near, O Lord, And all Thy
> commandments are truth."

Truth transcends time and cultures. What Christians believe and how they live will tell you something about his/her understanding of truth. Christians should find freedom in truth, because the foundation for truth is based on God's ultimate authority, the Word of God. In God's truth the child of God will find freedom and courage to follow the ways of the Lord. The strength from God's truth will make us stand straight. In the face of danger, God's people stand ready to delight in the Word of God.

8. Relief From Ridicule

Remember the Word to Your servant, upon which You have caused me to hope. This is my comfort in my affliction, for Your Word has given me life. The proud have me in great derision, Yet I do not turn aside from Your law. I remembered Your judgments of old, O LORD, and have comforted myself. Indignation has taken hold of me because of the wicked, who forsake Your law. Your statutes have been my songs in the house of my pilgrimage. I remember Your name in the night, O LORD, and I keep Your law. This has become mine, because I kept Your precepts.

Psalm 119:49-56

It is a curious notion that many professing Christians act as if they are utterly ignorant of the Word of God. I visited a congregation recently and the preacher was a well-respected seminary president. He spoke with certainty about the sad condition of the evangelical churches in the United States. Without any fear of ridicule he referred to "stupid saints" in the church. Specifically his reference was to long time church attenders who should be skilled in the Word of God. They should have the joy of knowing the Word of God as the rule of faith and life and humbly living according to the Word of God. However, his opinion was that the majority of professing evangelical Christians are basically ignorant of the teaching found in the Bible.

I am perplexed that there is so much ignorance of the Word of God in a country overflowing with Bibles and biblical literature. If a person attends worship regularly for 25 years, he or she would have heard over 1000 sermons, if they only attended one service a week. If they heard two sermons each week that would be 2,000 sermons, which does not include Sunday School lessons, group Bible study, and individual Bible study. Religious education is in great abundance in this country, yet some preachers refer to the majority of Christians as "stupid saints."

I expect it is largely because professing Christians have forgotten what they should remember. Have you ever heard the expression, "Remember the Alamo?" That saying is attributed to Colonel Sidney Sherman. After the Mexican President Santa Anna captured the Alamo and killed all the occupants, Santa Anna set out to snuff out the Lone Star Republic. But the battle of San Jacinto proved to be the defeat of Santa Anna. It was there that the Colonel told the Texans "Remember the Alamo!" This is an apt analogy for the Christian. But the Christian war cry is, "Remember the Word of God."

There are many reasons to remember the Word of God, but one particular reason is to find relief from ridicule. It is the Word of God accompanied by the Spirit of God that gives the child of God hope in this sinful world. However, God's people experience oppression from the evil in this world. The Psalmist talks about the affliction, derision, and indignation he suffered during his life on earth. Every Christian must face the truth. The apostle Paul wrote the church and warned them, "all who desire to live godly in Christ Jesus will suffer persecution." The Lord Jesus Christ said, "If the world hates you, you know that it hated Me before it hated you" (John 15:18). Jesus also said, "If they persecuted Me, they will also persecute you" (John 15:20). Notice, they attack "you" not the doctrine of Scripture. According to Acts the apostles were beaten because they preached the gospel of Christ. The apostles rejoiced that they were counted worthy to suffer shame for His name (Acts 5:41).

I agree with Jonathan Edwards when he said, "Reproaches and the malice and envy of the wicked may also be reckoned as some of the chief troubles of the godly" (Sermons and

Discourses, 1723-1729, Yale edition, vol. 14, p. 106). If Christians are not suffering persecution from the evil one, something is wrong, and it certainly is not the Word of God. When wicked despicable people persecute you "remember the Word of God." The wicked man forsakes the Word of God which compounds the guilt that is already overwhelming. His only recourse is to lash out with displeasure and oppression because the godly man has peace. The godly man finds comfort from the Word of God during times of persecution. To emphasize the importance of the Word of God, the Psalmist even said, "Your Word has given me life." When you find yourself hated and despised by wicked men, you must go to the Word of God to find comfort.

Even though Christians find comfort from God's Word, they still ask why the wicked unbelievers persecute the church. The eyes of believers are opened when they understand the Word of God so that their desire corresponds to God's Word. One of the obvious reasons that wicked men persecute God's Children is holiness of life. By holiness of life, I simply mean that a person endeavors to live according to God's Word. As the apostle Paul stated it, the Word of God captivates the Christian mind. The sad tragedy is that professing believers have been fed a heavy diet saturated with moralism and pietism. Moralism is a worldview. The following is my definition of Moralism.

> This worldview adopted by many evangelicals tends to make moral perfection the Christian standard for salvation. Moralism belongs to the doctrine of sanctification. The biblical doctrine of sanctification teaches that justification by faith alone breaks the dominion of sin, but sin is not eradicated. Self-righteousness is the platform for moralism. It is the modern concept for perfectionism. The Christian

> worldview is moral, but not perfect. (*Theological Terms in Layman Language*, by Martin Murphy, p. 70)

Pietism is a religious worldview. Their expressions of worship and duty toward God are self-motivated and regulated by unbiblical tradition. Moralism and pietism does not lead to a life of holiness and trust in God.

If the Word of God is taken seriously, persecution occurs. An exponential factor may be involved, because the more serious you take the Word of God the more the persecution. Persecution often comes because of conflicting belief systems. Another reason that wicked men persecute Christians is because they hate God, but they can't get their hands on God. They can get their hands and you, so you become the object of derision. "All those who see me ridicule me; They shoot out the lip, they shake the head, saying He trusted in the Lord" (Psalm 22:7).

The cruel mocking described in Psalm 22 reminds us of the universal scorn and ridicule of the Lord Jesus Christ. Think of all the ridicule and laughter poured out on the Lord Jesus Christ. The priests and most of the Jews, Gentiles, and soldiers scoffed at Him as He was about to die for the sake of God's people. Finally the suffering Savior was taunted because of His faith in God. Wicked men will try to make your life as bitter and miserable as possible with their seemingly interminable temptation. Suffering and persecution comes from the hands of wicked men who hate you, but the Word of God promises life. The wicked man anticipates death, while the godly man has assurance of life. Wicked men are proud men. Pride is a root sin. From it many sins abound. The Bible makes it clear that the proud man is not in a favorable relationship with God. "God resists the proud, but gives grace to the humble" (James 4:6). The word "pride" in Scripture most often refers to one who puts himself above others. He thinks that he is more important than others. He wants people to look up to him. He is one who thinks that his opinion is above all others.

The foundation upon which a proud man builds his life is indeed shaky and will for certain crumble in the end. One of the greatest monarchs to live on earth was Nebuchadnezzar, but notice what happened to the great proud Nebuchadnezzar. "But when his heart was lifted up (Nebuchadnezzar's) and his spirit was hardened in pride, he was deposed from his kingly throne, and they took his glory from him" (Daniel 5:20). Temporary glory is no glory at all. Wicked proud men ridicule the humble children of God because pride is built on Satan's launching pad. John Calvin commenting on first Corinthians said, "Where pride is, there is ignorance of God." Pride is naturally blind, because it is part of man's natural sinful estate. "The natural man does not receive the things of the Spirit of God, for they are foolishness to him; nor can he know them, because they are spiritually discerned" (1 Corinthians 2:14).

Glory, honor, esteem, dignity, and majesty belong to God, not to men. It is when men desire to act like God that they find themselves filled with pride. Self-love and the ambition to be noticed by men are the marks of pride. Such a man will be resisted by God. Proud men shelter themselves in the name of a church, all the while robbing God of the praise due His name. The unconverted sinner amuses himself with various ideas, thinking that he might dismiss the coming judgment of God. So they put on a front. Image is everything and substance is zero. The heart of an unconverted sinner is so hardened that he applauds his own sin.

So where does this leave the church? If an unbeliever remains outside the church, his boasting and flattery is to his own disgrace. However, if a church member "boasts in appearance and not in heart" his boasting and flattery is to the disgrace of the church.

When a church member flatters himself too much the ministry of the church will suffer. All too often the sin in the church today is the same as it was at Corinth. The strife, bickering, and contention enlarge so that the ministry of the church suffers.

Christians can be certain that God is not the friend of the proud man and in the end the proud shall see God as their enemy. God's people must remember the words of Jesus Christ as He explains, "whoever humbles himself as this little child is the greatest in the kingdom of heaven" (Matthew 18:4). John Calvin commented on that verse in Matthew with these words.

> Man is truly humble who never claims any personal merit in the sight of God, nor proudly despises brethren, or aims at being thought superior to them, but reckons it enough that he is one of the members of Christ and desires nothing more than that Christ alone should be exalted. (*John Calvin Commentary* on Matthew 18:4)

Remember the Word of God when the proud man ridicules you. Keep the Word of God before you at all times. What an appropriate exercise for Christians to remember the name of the Lord.

Rejection is a terrible blow to self-esteem, but Christians must not lose sight of their purpose. Christians have a unique purpose. It is to glorify God and enjoy perfect peace with Him forever. Enjoy God's goodness and love anticipating eternal felicity with God. Christians have peace and comfort, because they have the Word of God. Relief from ridicule is certain when Christians stand with integrity because the Word of God is the true witness. We must ask the question: "What did the Psalmist gain in maintaining integrity to God's Word." All he said was, "This has become mine." Essentially the Psalmist claimed ownership to the Word of God. Do you own the Word of God? If you claim ownership to the Word of God, it will change everything about you. You have the Word of God to justify everything you think and practice. Let God be your witness, as he reveals His Word to you by the power of His Spirit. While the proud wicked man stands on his own honor, you, my Christian friend, stand upon the Word of God.

The only way to experience God's saving grace is to have the Word of God your rule of faith and practice.

The only way to get understanding is from the Word of God.

The only way to find comfort in affliction is from the Word of God.

The only way to be filled with joy and peace is to let God's Word be your word.

The only way to find meaning in life is from the Word of God.

The Psalmist said Your Word has given me life……….

Can you honestly say, "The Word of God has given me life?" It is a question we must all answer with sobriety and honesty.

9. Life After Conversion

You are my portion, O LORD; I have said that I would keep Your Words. I entreated Your favor with my whole heart; be merciful to me according to Your Word. I thought about my ways, and turned my feet to Your testimonies. I made haste, and did not delay to keep Your commandments. The cords of the wicked have bound me, but I have not forgotten Your law. At midnight I will rise to give thanks to You, because of Your righteous judgments. I am a companion of all who fear You, and of those who keep Your precepts. The earth, O LORD, is full of Your mercy; Teach me Your statutes.

Psalm 119:57-64

Martin and Mary were recently married and shortly after marriage, the couple had a single friend ask the question: "What is life like after marriage?" Martin had a friend ask the question: "What is life like since retirement?" Likewise an unbeliever might ask: "What is life like after conversion?" People tend to trust sense experience as the ultimate source of truth and by extension the ultimate authority for life. Christians, on the other hand, have the Word of God for all of faith and life.

Believers have assurance of grace and salvation without having to see the death of the Lord Jesus Christ. The Word of God makes promises regarding assurance of salvation. However, deep down inside there may be the remnant of skepticism. Christians may ask, "how do I know I have assurance of salvation?" If the question infers the metaphysical (the existence that follows death), then we will find most everyone is a skeptic at some time or the other to some degree or the other.

With all the seriousness of life, death, and eternity, God's people should take pleasure in the doctrine of assurance. It is important to every Christian because the doctrine of assurance teaches that the Christian is in a state of grace and a favorable relationship with God. The doctrine of assurance is necessary to know and experience the certainty of the state of grace and the certainty of having a favorable relationship with God. The Bible teaches that evidence accompanies true assurance (Colossians 2:2). It is sad, but true that many professing Christians find false assurance in their own beliefs and their feelings based on human experience apart from the Word of God. Conjecture is never a reason to believe something is real. In the case of assurance of salvation, feelings and emotional sensations will never stand before the bar of eternal justice. The Bible teaches that many men deceive themselves into believing that they are in a state of grace and in a right relationship with God.

One Christian confession says that "hypocrites, and other unregenerate men, may vainly deceive themselves with false hopes and carnal presumptions" (*Westminster Confession of Faith*, 18.1). False assurance is less certain in the mind of many professing Christians than true assurance. It always has been. "Her heads judge for a bribe, Her priests teach for pay, and her prophets divine for money, yet they lean on the Lord and say, is not the Lord among us? No harm can come upon us?" (Micah 3:11). False assurance was just as popular in the Old Testament as it is today.

True assurance does belong to those who " truly believe in the Lord Jesus, and love Him in sincerity, endeavoring to walk in all good conscience before Him" (*Doctrine of Sound Words*, by Martin Murphy, p. 109). The Bible asserts that Christians may know they have assurance. "These things I have written to you who believe in the name of the Son of God, that you may know that you have eternal life, and that you may continue to believe in the name of the Son of God" (1 John 5:13).

When God renewed His covenant with the Israelites in the land of Moab, God warned His people.

> So that there may not be among you man or woman or family or tribe, whose heart turns away today from the Lord our God, to go and serve the gods of these nations, and that there may not be among you a root bearing bitterness or wormwood; and so it may not happen, when he hears the words of this curse, that he blesses himself in his heart, saying, 'I shall have peace, even though I follow the dictates of my heart'—as though the drunkard could be included with the sober. (Deuteronomy 29:18-19)

It is sad indeed when people believe they have peace with God when in reality they are at war with God. The Lord Jesus Christ does not mince words on the issue of deceptive men who are without assurance of grace and salvation. The Lord said, "Beware of the false prophets, who come to you in sheep's clothing, but inwardly are ravenous wolves"(Matthew 7:15). False assurance will face reality because the Lord said, "Many will say to Me on that day, (the day of judgment) 'Lord, Lord, did we not prophesy in Your name, and in Your name cast out demons, and in Your name perform many miracles" (Matthew 7:22). The reference to "many" implies a large number. Also in the context of Matthew chapter seven, the large number refers to a large number in the church. The Words of Jesus Christ make it ring loud and clear that there is a large number in the church of Jesus Christ who are deceived in themselves. The words "false prophets" as Jesus used them does not merely refer to someone speaking of future events. In fact, a biblical prophet is someone who simply speaks forth. A false prophet is someone who speaks a lie with every intention to deceive and destroy with those lies. It is clear from the whole of Scripture that the false prophet is an enemy of God;

therefore the false prophet is a man who is not in a state of grace or a favorable relationship with God. The false prophet has false assurance. On the day of judgment the Lord Jesus Christ, the Judge of heaven and earth will say, "I never knew you; DEPART FROM ME, you who practice lawlessness" (Matthew 7:23).

An atheist should expect to hear those words, but those who profess the Christian religion should not expect to hear those words, but as Jesus said, "many" will hear those words. To the professing Christian who is actually an unbeliever, those words from the mouth of Jesus Christ may seem harsh and unloving. To the professing believer who is actually a Christian, those words should simply be a reminder to examine their own condition before the final examination. The first reason given by the Psalmist that gives him assurance of grace and salvation is what he believes about His relationship with the Lord.

The Psalmist expressed his assurance in familial terms. "The Lord is my inheritance" (Psalm 119:57). It was the Lord's choice to give the Psalmist an inheritance - an eternal inheritance. The Psalmist was then pleased to receive the inheritance by believing the Lord. However, it is presumptuous to believe that the Psalmist never struggled with the assurance of his eternal inheritance. As all sinful men, the Psalmist did struggle and have doubts. He was tempted by sin and the various miseries that accompany sin. "But as for me, my feet had almost stumbled; My steps had nearly slipped" (Psalm 73:2). The Psalmist had confidence in the Word of God. "You will guide me with Your counsel, and afterward receive me to glory" (Psalm 73:24).

The Christian's desire in life is certainly a desire for good. They must desire God for He is the ultimate good. The Lord Jesus Christ said, "there is none good but one; that is God" (Matthew 19:17). God is the highest good. He is infinitely and permanently good.

God gives His people the ultimate authority, the Word of God, so they may stand against doubt and skepticism. When spiritual struggles cause you to doubt your inheritance, ask the Lord to be merciful according to the Word of God.

If Christians believe God is their portion, then the right question should be applied personally. Do you actually believe that you are in a right relationship with the Lord? If you were to suddenly pass from this life and appear before the Lord, would he say, "Good and well done faithful servant?" If your answer is yes, then you must test your answer. The test is whether or not you were resolved to believe and obey the Word of the Lord.

One of the evidences that God is your inheritance is that you pray for His favor with your whole heart. Christians must desire God's grace. If you desire God's grace, then your desire is God's will; therefore, you desire the Word of God and the Word of God becomes fruitful in your life with Jesus Christ.

Another evidence of your eternal inheritance is you want to know God and know about Him. You must desire to have some understanding about who He is and what He does. Doubts, fears, and uncertainty of the unseen will often keep Christians from knowing God in His fullness.

Scripture speaks openly and abundantly about the psychological aspects of doubt, fear and uncertainty. "Remember now your Creator in the days of your youth, before the difficult days come, and the years draw near when you say, 'I have no pleasure in them'" (Ecclesiastes 12:1).

The time may come when you will not find pleasure, joy and peace in your soul. Life may seem like a burden. Then you must find God's prize which is His mercy according to His Word. Overcoming those doubts, fears, and uncertainty is a matter of praying and asking God to be gracious according to His Word. "Let us therefore draw near with confidence to the throne of grace, that we may receive mercy and may find grace to help in time of need" (Hebrews 4:16).

God promised by a blood covenant to save His people. However absolute and certain that promise is, it is not to be taken with a grain of salt. The one professing the true religion must examine himself or herself and see if there is any reason to be assured of grace and salvation through self-examination. A believer should study his or her own life to see if it is aligned with the Word of God.

Christians ought to be quick to obey the Word of God. Reforming the sinful estate is often a difficult, slow and tedious endeavor. Yet the man of God shows and confirms His relationship with God by conscientiously turning to the Word of God and obeying the Word of God.

Christians live among wicked people and wicked people will often try to harass the church. One of the most difficult challenges for Christians is obedience during persecution. Yet one of the signs of grace and salvation is endurance during the time of suffering and persecution. In the darkest hour of suffering and persecution the man of God will remember to give thanks to the Lord. If we believe the whole counsel of God, that is the whole Word of God, we must believe that God ordained suffering and persecution. The child of God should take advantage of God's ultimate authority during the time of suffering and persecution.

To say that a person can act wickedly, live a despicable life, and make mockery of the Word of God and still have assurance of grace and salvation is the most foolish of all thoughts. If professing Christians want to have assurance and confidence in God's saving grace, they must call out to God and say, "Teach me Your Word." If God provides the instruction and professing Christians do not listen, they should go the Lord and pray for His grace and mercy. If you belong to Jesus Christ you have every reason to have assurance of salvation and eternal life, because those reasons are found in the Word of God.

10. The Real is not Deceptive

You have dealt well with Your servant, O Lord, according to Your Word. Teach me good judgment and knowledge, for I believe Your commandments. Before I was afflicted I went astray, but now I keep Your Word. You are good, and do good; Teach me Your statutes. The proud have forged a lie against me, but I will keep Your precepts with my whole heart. Their heart is as fat as grease, but I delight in Your law. It is good for me that I have been afflicted, that I may learn Your statutes. The law of Your mouth is better to me than thousands of coins of gold and silver.

Psalm 119:65-72

The meaning of life is measured by understanding reality. This is true both morally and aesthetically. The way we live morally must be grounded in reality. The way we see the world around us must have meaning. True beauty (aesthetics) must be real to have meaning. Likewise, ethics must be real to have meaning.

Those things, which are real, make sense. The fake things of this world do not make sense. If we pretend something *is* when that something *is not*, we deceive ourselves. If I said I was an airplane pilot, I'm deceiving myself and if I told someone else that I was an airplane pilot, I'd be deceiving them. I know people who pretend that they have financial independence and wealth when it is not true. Pretense is deception. Deception is anything that denies reality. Deception is merely a mask. Deception is a fake. It is presumptuous and outright dangerous to pretend anything, but especially dangerous when the soul is the object of reality.

The connection between reality and how reality relates to the soul of man is found in almost every verse of Psalm 119.

Do you know what connects the soul of man with reality? It is the Word of God. It is the Word of God that defines and prescribes the faith and practice for Christians. The Word of God defines and prescribes what Christians are to believe concerning God. The Word of God defines and prescribes what Christians are to do in their relationship to God. Without question, the Word of God is the centerpiece for understanding the world that is really real. The Psalmist was uniquely acquainted with the Word of God, affirmed in Psalm 119:

> I look into all your commandments - Verse 6
> I will not forget your Word - Verse 16
> I have chosen the way of truth - Verse 30
> I trust in your Word - Verse 42

The Word of God is real to everyone who is in a favorable relation with God through Jesus Christ by the power of the Holy Spirit. Christians see life through the glasses of reality, rather than hiding behind the mask of deceit.

The reality of God's goodness is evident, but sometimes people miss seeing the obvious. Sometimes they miss the profound reality of some obvious truth because they may be blinded by the simplicity of it. For that reason the goodness of God is abundantly clear according to the Word of God. The interest of the sinful flesh cannot see the goodness of God during times of sickness or during a time of poverty or during any other misery brought on because of sin. The sinful nature causes Christians to draw an image of God that discredits His goodness. The sinful nature in man distorts reality so that even a truly converted Christian may find it difficult, at various times to offer thanksgiving to God for His goodness. Yet it was a deep and abiding appreciation for the Word of God that brought thanksgiving to the tongue of the Psalmist. Thankfulness should be on the tip of the tongue of every Christian. The pious pretension that prevails may be found in mere superficial clichés like, "Are you in the Word brother" or "Has the Word spoken to you today?" I'm not sure what those clichés mean because more often than not I find professing Christians talking about personal experiences rather than the Word of God. Personal experiences are important, but personal experience must be measured in relation to the Word of God to determine whether or not those experiences are really real. When Christians experience the goodness of God, they are filled with a heart of thankfulness.

Affliction represents pain and suffering. Sin is the root cause of affliction and the result is real and painful misery in this life. Afflictions will certainly continue throughout life without the saving work of Jesus Christ powerfully applied by the Spirit to the souls of men. Affliction should not be ignored, because actually affliction is good. Affliction is also good especially for Christians, because it keeps them on the right path. God's people are prone to wander as the prophet Jeremiah said, "they have loved to wander; they have not restrained their feet" (Jeremiah 14:10). Affliction is not just good, it is necessary for salvation. God uses affliction to humble men, which in turn causes men to think about God.

> We are hard-pressed on every side, yet not crushed; we are perplexed, but not in despair; persecuted, but not forsaken; struck down, but not destroyed—always carrying about in the body the dying of the Lord Jesus, that the life of Jesus also may be manifested in our body" (2 Corinthians 4:8-10). Paul goes so far to say, "we exult in our tribulations." (New American Standard Version, Romans 5:3)

Christians have to be careful not to become martyrs for the hope of salvation. Affliction cannot save anyone, but afflictions should remind Christians of their weakness, frailty and inability to save themselves. There are times that God may send the affliction for a purpose. Affliction should drive Christians to the Word of God. The Psalmist said, "It is good for me that I have been afflicted, that I may learn Your statutes" (Psalm 119:71). So we, like the Psalmist, are to offer thanksgiving to God for the fiery furnace of affliction, because those afflictions send us to the Word of God. It is in the Word of God that one will find reality. Without the Word of God, the Son of God cannot be known as the Savior of God's children. Without the Word of God ethics and morality are simply matters of preference.

No one can make anyone go to the Word of God, to meet reality, but they should be warned of the dangers if they fail to listen to God's Word. The prevailing danger and the most formidable enemy of reality is deception. The news media has become the monstrous ally of deception. It is said, tongue and cheek I hope, that the words of a news anchor is like god speaking. However, they often take comments out of context and speak with the skill of a sophist. Many politicians use deceptive tactics to get laws passed. For instance, they allege that guns are the cause of violence, when in reality it is the person using the gun that is the cause of violence. Educators have become master deceivers with the new postmodern language, commonly called deconstructionism. Religious leaders are just as guilty. They harbor heresy. They promote pragmatism. Unfortunately on many occasions they reject the clear teaching of Scripture.

Christians must not ignore the pride of ungodly deceivers. "The proud have forged (or shaped) a lie against me" (Psalm 119:69). Pride is an enemy of truth. The ungodly proud man sets out to destroy the character of godly humble Christian. The weapon of destruction is a lie against the godly man. Slander is deception and if you defend the Word of God, you are likely to be slandered. With the advent of postmodern principles, truth has been removed from the public square. Children are taught to believe, speak, and follow the deception of the evil in this world. Deception has become a comfortable way of life causing children to lose sight of reality.

In contrast to deception there is equity and dignity, both of which are very real, both of which are found in the Word of God. There is equity in the saving work of the Lord Jesus Christ. There is dignity in the character of those who love and obey the Lord Jesus Christ according to the Word of God.

The Word of God is more important than all the riches of this world. The material wealth of this world may very well deceive the collective church. Riches are not inherently evil, but riches may be very deceptive. "Happy is the man who finds wisdom, and the man who gains understanding; For her proceeds are better than the profits of silver, and her gain than fine gold" (Proverbs 3:13,14). The place to gain wisdom and improve our understanding is from the Word of God.

Christians ought to consider the difference between true riches and counterfeit riches. Apply that distinction personally. You have true riches when God is your portion. You have true riches when you have Jesus Christ as your redeemer. You have true riches when you have the Holy Spirit as your sanctifier and comforter.

Counterfeit riches are those things which belong to this world such as money, land, stocks, cares, guns, and so on. They are counterfeit riches because they are deceptive. The things of this world draw us away from the things of God. The parable of the rich man in Luke is an example of deceptive riches. "You fool this very night your soul is required of you and now who will own what you have prepared" (See Luke 12:11-21). The riches of this world are insignificant relative to the riches of the eternal soul favored with God's grace.

A child of God will find more treasure in one book of the Bible than the ungodly will find in all the riches of this life. For that reason the Psalmist prayed for God to teach him good judgment and knowledge. The only place he could find those things is in the Word of God. It is in the Word of God that you will find reality in the true meaning of pardon of sin, God's redemptive plan, and the grace of the Lord Jesus Christ.

The Real is Not Deceptive!

11. Prayer According to God's Word

Your hands have made me and fashioned me; Give me under-standing, that I may learn Your commandments. Those who fear You will be glad when they see me, because I have hoped in Your Word. I know, O Lord, that Your judgments are right, and that in faithfulness You have afflicted me. Let, I pray, Your merciful kindness be for my comfort, according to Your Word to Your servant. Let Your tender mercies come to me, that I may live; For Your law is my delight. Let the proud be ashamed, for they treated me wrongfully with falsehood; But I will meditate on Your precepts. Let those who fear You turn to me, those who know Your testimonies. Let my heart be blame-less regarding Your statutes, that I may not be ashamed.
Psalm 119:73-80

Several years ago a friend asked me to join a local internet discussion board. I was acquainted with a few people on the discussion board and I frequently visited the site. The majority of those who posted on the board showed no evidence of professing faith in Christ. Actually, most of them criticized the church and mocked the Christian religion. However, when one among them became ill or had a tragedy in life, someone would ask for prayers and the board would light up with comments primarily consisting of comments like "prayers up." All of a sudden there was something up in the sky that they perceived would help them in the time of need.

Psalm 119 is the Christian guide to prayer. It is specifically a guide to pray according to the Word of God. The prayer of the Psalmist ought to be the prayer of every Christian. "Let, I pray, Your merciful kindness be for my comfort, according to Your Word to Your servant" (Psalm 119:76). The Bible is an abundant store for Christians to follow in their prayer life.

Christians pray to God because He is the source of all being. Since human beings are dependent creatures, by necessity they appeal to the independent Creator. The Psalmist starts his prayer with a confession. "Your hands have made me and fashioned me" (Psalm 119:73). Christians realize that the divine hand of God had a purpose in creation. More specifically, God had a personal interest in every human being by making them with His own hands. God molded us so that our shape in existence has meaning and personality. The Bible clearly explains that we are created in God's image. God created the human personality with a mind to think, a will to decide, and with emotions to express what the mind thinks and the will decides.

Paul explained this concept to the philosophers at Athens by explaining that God made the world and all things in it and He Himself gives to all life and breath. (See Acts 17:24-28.)

If Christians expect to make sense out of the world they live in, they have to understand who they are in their relationship with God. Therefore, they should pray as the Psalmist prayed to the Lord, "Give me understanding, that I may learn Your commandments" (Psalm 119:73).

Christians would be wise to listen to the inspired Psalmist because the prayer in Psalm 119 is the prayer of a persecuted man. It is the school of testing, trials and affliction that bring Christians face to face with God. A persecuted man will either be humbled before God or the persecuted man will shake his fist in God's face. The former belongs to the household of faith. The latter belongs to the evil one.

The prayer requests (plural) in Psalm 119:73 - 80 are all important, but their end is the same, that the Psalmist may know and act according to the Word of God. The Psalmist begins his prayer request in the form of a command to the Lord, "Give me understanding." This is a recurring notion in the mind of the Psalmist. He uses the same identical request to God five different times in Psalm 119. Why so often? What is wrong with the Psalmist? Does he have a learning disability? When the Psalmist cries to God for understanding, the Psalmist does not intend to ask for knowledge. The Psalmist wants the Lord to give him the ability to discern. Knowledge is not discernment. The inspired writer of Proverbs will help us understand the meaning the Psalmist attaches to the word understanding.

The inspired writer of Proverbs explains this very important doctrine. "The discerning heart seeks knowledge" (Proverbs 15:14). Knowledge is not useful without discernment and knowledge may be outright destructive. Knowledge improperly interpreted turns into deceit, lies, and sophistry. This doctrine may be directly applied to professing Christians in this present age. There is a sense in which Christians know too much. They have a large body of knowledge. They may be able to quote Scripture. They may repeat a confession of faith.

Sometimes knowledge is a dangerous thing. In fact, I would venture to say that knowledge without discernment or without understanding will create a monster. I will never forget these words of a retired Presbyterian minister: "Many professing Christians have way too much Bible knowledge." His point was Christians do not apply the knowledge for the sake of the mission and ministry of the church. Sometimes Bible knowledge causes more confusion in the church. For instance, the Bible teaches God our Savior desires all men to be saved. The Bible also teaches that the rich man was in Hades, in Hell suffering eternal torment. It sounds as if God has an unfulfilled desire, which desecrates the character of God. There is a problem with that body of knowledge. The limited body of knowledge is in contradiction. Any way you go with the argument or any way you try to explain the contradiction, you end up with a nonsense proposition. The harder you try to explain the nonsense, the more tangled up your web becomes.

Discernment is absolutely necessary for harmony, order, and clarity to prevail. Adam was created with the ability to make decisions without knowledge corrupting his decision making process. When Adam sinned his mind still functioned, but speculative knowledge was his plight. Speculative knowledge includes the notion of consciousness without intelligence.

God has given us a mind. It is part of our personality. A mind without the grace of God is nothing more than a wicked personality. Satan has a mind, but it is wicked. It is perverted. It is devious in all its thoughts. It is a mind that is absent of God's grace.

The apostle Paul instructed God's people to, "be transformed by the renewing of your mind, that you may prove what the will of God is, that which is good and acceptable and perfect" (Romans 12:2). Paul was a believer and the Psalmist was a believer, but they both needed understanding. The Bible makes it abundantly clear that Christians must be discerning. They must make judicious decisions for the purpose of understanding the Word of God.

God created man for the purpose of understanding God's holiness, not to usurp God's righteous character. It pleases God to give His people an interest in Him so they may worship and adore Him. Jesus Christ is the ultimate interest for believers. They have a renewed mind because of His interest in them. The Psalmist was so zealous for understanding. He was a troubled man and he needed the insight of a holy, all-powerful God to give him assurance.

Even with Christ as our Savior we are troubled people, but we have something that those who are without Christ do not have. We have His Spirit and His Word. The bitterness we taste in this world of troubles and persecution will turn to sweetness when God gives us understanding from the Word of God. The Psalmist didn't just believe "he knew" that God was righteous and that God was faithful. His confidence was in the

Word of God, not the word of man. The arrogant, haughty, proud, sinful man will be put to shame, but the man of God prays for redemption. Living in a troubled world is not easy. When people accuse you without a cause it is troubling - it is a form of persecution.

The source of much trouble is a lying heart. We will do well to remember the words of the Lord Jesus Christ; Satan is a liar and the father of lies. The wicked man described in Psalm 119 is a liar with a purpose. As the New American Standard Version has it, "the arrogant subvert me with a lie." Liars bend the truth out of shape. Then they can attack the character of God's people. You can't change the mind of evil men, only God can do that. What you can do is pray that the wicked might see their need for Christ. If the Holy Spirit changes the heart, they will desire the Word of God.

The Psalmist prayed for an unrelenting, blameless, unwavering adherence to the Word of God. Blameless does not mean sinless perfection, but it does mean we have a perfect rule to follow in the Word of God. The Psalmist prays that his heart will be so full of the law of God or the Word of God that he will not have room to tell a lie.

When the troubles of this world persecute you, turn to the Lord God who made you and pray for understanding. Pray that God will comfort you in your afflictions. Pray that the ungodly liar will be ashamed of his sin. Pray that your heart will be filled with the Word of God.

12. Secular Life

My soul faints for Your salvation, but I hope in Your Word. My eyes fail from searching Your Word, saying, "When will You comfort me?" For I have become like a wineskin in smoke, yet I do not forget Your statutes. How many are the days of Your servant? When will You execute judgment on those who persecute me? The proud have dug pits for me, which is not according to Your law. All Your commandments are faithful; They persecute me wrongfully; Help me! They almost made an end of me on earth, but I did not forsake Your precepts. Revive me according to Your lovingkindness, so that I may keep the testimony of Your mouth.

Psalm 119: 81-88

Leaders among professing evangelicals are talking about "an increasingly secular world." The concept of an increasingly secular world is a trend that preachers use to satisfy the discontentment of professing Christians looking for the answers to the complex questions in life. The 911 attacks by Muslim terrorists on the United States provoked many alleged Christian preachers to address the moral dilemma of this country. People were asking the question: "Why did God allow that evil atrocity to take place in NYC?" One popular nationally known preacher blamed the attacks on abortionists, feminists, homosexuals, the American Civil Liberties Union and the People for the American Way. He went on to say, "All of them who have tried to secularize America, I point the finger in their face and say you helped this happen." I withhold his name because this not about personalities, it's about principles. The often used phrase, "secularize America" is an impossible notion. The word "secular" essentially refers to that which is worldly or temporal. It is the "present time" or the "here and now" and does not include the "eternal." It means to live in this present world without reference to the theological doctrine of an eternal existence. No one can be more or less secular, because everyone lives at the present time and that is what it means to be secular. Unfortunately professing Christian leaders use that kind of language.

Seminary professors tell their students to preach practical sermons touching the hearts of the people, so they will have a better secular life. Under the guise of the gospel the goal is to instruct people so that the complexities of life will be easier to handle on a day to day basis. The evangelical church has adopted this mass of false teaching from celebrity preachers and charlatans. Many skilled theologians know better, but they remain silent for the sake of unity. A sample of what you may expect from preachers graduating from seminary comes from the mouth of a seminary professor. One professor said: "If a preacher wants to be heard, he must diligently encourage his people to think about themselves, their lives and value systems, their responsibilities and destinies and of course God."

> Think about self – secular self
> Think about life – secular life
> Think about value systems – secular values
> Think about responsibilities – secular responsibilities

Thank goodness he finally added "destiny and God." The professor described the world as it has always existed since the sin of our father Adam. It is a man-centered world. The world is not becoming increasingly secular. If anything the world is becoming increasingly sinful. There is a radical difference between the two, but at the same time the sinful life and the secular life are common to each other. All too often professing believers do not seek the glory of God, but on the contrary the church runs after the wisdom of wicked men from this secular world. The church should be saddened because there is so much disregard for the Word of God. It is the Word of God that holds forth the glory of God in all His majesty and dignity. It is the Word of God that explains the way of salvation to sinners.

This secular world is complex. God's people need to go to the right place if they expect to understand the complexities of life. The right place is the Word of God. Psalm 119 affirms what Christians believe to be true about life. It affirms the reality of daily trials and tribulations. It graphically explains the secular world of ancient times, of which explanation they can readily relate. At the same time it tells them where to go for hope and assurance of a glorious ending for the people of God.

The Psalmist finds the secular world distressing because of the wickedness in the world. He confesses his need and prays to be vindicated based on his understanding of God's Word. Living in the secular time with all its sin and misery is reason enough to search the sacred Word.

The Psalmist cries out with words like, "My eyes fail from searching Your Word, saying, "When will you comfort me?" The Christian may cry out with words like, "Lord I'm reading the Bible and I find hope, encouragement, and assurance on every page, a truth I cannot deny, but my trials and tribulations overwhelm me."

The inspired Word of God says to, "Consider it all joy, my brethren, when you encounter various trials, knowing that the testing of your faith produces endurance" (James 1:2-3). The Bible does not say, "if you encounter trails" but "you will encounter trials." Understanding the source of trials and temptations will resolve much of the confusion.

> Let no one say when he is tempted, "I am being tempted by God"; for God cannot be tempted by evil, and He Himself does not tempt anyone. But each one

is tempted when he is carried away and enticed by his own lust. (James 1:13-14)

James makes it clear that trials are part of life. God is sovereign and finds pleasure in sending trials to put the Christian's profession of faith to the test. Christians face a variety of trials in this life. What seems to be a trial for one person is not a trial for another. Every Christian has trials, some of which are incidental and others are trials because of sin. Trials are not uncommon, but they may be dangerous because they may become temptations. Before trials turn into temptations, turn to the Word of God. When Christians face trials in this secular life, they ought to pray like the Psalmist prayed. "My eyes fail from searching Your Word, saying, 'When will You comfort me?' Yet I do not forget Your statutes" (Psalm 119:82-83).

The Psalmist does not doubt God's hand of deliverance, but only wonders when God will act. The Psalmist realizes that life is short and wants God to act quickly. Christians should desire to see the righteousness of Christ vindicated, but patience is the key word to remember.

Wicked men are instruments of testing and Christians want wicked men punished for their wicked ways. Wicked men persecuted the Psalmist. He suffered and expected the enemies of God to be judged and punished. The prayer of the Psalmist is not against any particular person and certainly no personalities are involved in this prayer.

Wicked men will test your faith. "The proud have dug pits for me, which is not according to Your law" (Psalm 119:85). The proud refers to wicked men. This is a common expression used in ancient times to describe the deceitful and dangerous ways of wicked men. This kind of language is typical in the Old Testament. The digging of the pit infers physical harm. Wicked ungodly men molested and murdered the only perfect man, Jesus Christ. Christians are persecuted without a cause.

"For without a cause they have hidden their net for me in a pit, which they have dug without cause for my life" (Psalm 35:7).

The enemies of the Psalmist were enemies of God. It naturally follows that the wicked are also enemies of the Word of God. The kind of behavior found in Psalm 119 by wicked men is directly opposed to the Word of God. Ungodly actions, secret plotting's against God's people, and deceitful maneuvering to hurt God's people are most despicable to God as evidenced in God's Word.

The pits and nets of wicked men are too many to mention, but a few will suffice to understand this important doctrine. Wicked men have set a trap to divide God's people. Nothing has hindered the growth of the Christian church more than divisions. The Puritan theologian, Thomas Manton has said, "divisions in the church breed atheism in the world." Christian history has endless examples of how effectively wicked men divided the people of God. Destructive unbelievers have always plagued the church. Julian the Apostate is a good example. Julian the apostate did not openly persecute the church. He tried to plant people in the church to create division. He used others to quarrel and dispute with God's people. The outward effect was discord and division.

Another pit used by wicked men is ignorance. Wicked men have always used the ignorance of others to gainfully employ the professing believer to the work of Satan.

The pits of the wicked men start with the shovel of pride. Plotting to create division among God's people may be traced to the pride of unbelieving wicked men. When Christians are wrongfully persecuted they should ask God for patience and wisdom. Pray that the pits of division and ignorance will be overcome. Christians need the Spirit of God so they can understand the Word of God. If they understand the Word of God, they must repent of the pride that so easily overtakes them. If Christians envy those whom God has placed over them, then pride has overtaken them. Self-esteem may try to replace God. If Christians look disparagingly toward those who are without the gifts given to the Christians, then pride has overtaken them.

When our souls wish for deliverance from those troubles and afflictions in this secular world, we should find hope in the Word of God. It is from the Word of God that we find the gospel, filled with the saving grace of the Lord Jesus Christ. The wicked may dig pits for Christians, but Christians find their comfort, hope, and joy in the lovingkindness of God's favor according to His Word.

Christians must pray that God will revive the church according to His lovingkindness. "Many are the sorrows of the wicked; But he who trusts in the Lord, lovingkindness shall surround him" (Psalm 32:10). The lovingkindness of God belongs to the covenant people of God, not to any state or any nation. The lovingkindness of God shines upon the covenant people of God when the peace of Christ prevails.

The ultimate relief from the pain, suffering, and misery of this secular life is God's faithful promises to save His people according to His Word.

13. God Does Not Mutate

Forever, O Lord, Your Word is settled in heaven. Your faith-fulness endures to all generations; You established the earth, and it abides. They continue this day according to Your ordinances, for all are Your servants. Unless Your law had been my delight, I would then have perished in my affliction. I will never forget Your precepts, for by them You have given me life. I am Yours, save me; for I have sought Your precepts. The wicked wait for me to destroy me, but I will consider Your testimonies. I have seen the consummation of all perfection, but Your commandment is exceedingly broad.

Psalm 119:89-96

The great German scholar Franz Delitzsch explained that Psalm 119 consisted of complaints and consolations from an afflicted man. He describes the Psalmist as one in prison - imprisoned in a world of suffering. The complaints of the Psalmist were graphically real. Without the ultimate authority to guide and comfort him, the Psalmist declares, "I would then have perished in my affliction" (Psalm 119:92). Having total confidence in something greater than himself was enough to sustain his life. The Psalmist prayed that he might keep the Word of God.

The only way out of his suffering prison was to find some-thing that transcended his human experience and that was the Word of God. The experience of each day may confuse you or confound you, because human experience is at best sinful. Whether you are persecuted for the sake of Jesus Christ or if you face simple everyday trials, you must have the means to interpret and act upon your experience or trial. However it takes more than the Word of God.

The Spirit of God is necessary to believe and understand the Word of God. The renewing of the mind enables one to believe the Word of God is actually the voice of God. The will must be disinclined from sin and inclined toward holiness. The renewed soul will desire and search for an absolute standard to measure the new man. That absolute standard is the Word of God. The Word of God is to the soul what air is to the body. Without air the body will lose its life. Without the Word of God the soul will have no vitality.

The modern or the enlightened worldview tried to deify sense experience by scientific discovery and applying the principles of the scientific method to theology and philosophy. Modernity failed to give life to culture, so the cultural elites adopted a postmodern theory. The result was that the Word of God came under the critical eye of ungodly liberal theologians. Unfortunately their criticism was flawed by the sin of human experience. Soon enough the Word of God was no longer the Word of God. The postmodern way of life abandons all forms of criticism, especially literary, moral, or political. The postmodern posits a private subjective interpretive theory.

The modern and postmodern worldviews are hitching posts for humanism. The humanist agenda is open for the world to see. In fact, they define themselves very carefully. It is sad but true that many professing Christians are profoundly and significantly influenced by humanistic philosophy. A definition of humanism by the humanist accurately demonstrates their agenda.

> Humanism is a rational philosophy informed by science, inspired by art, and motivated by compassion. Affirming the dignity of each human being, it supports the maximization of individual liberty and opportunity consonant with social and planetary responsibility. It advocates the extension of participatory democracy

and the expansion of the open society, standing for human rights and social justice. Free of supernaturalism, it recognizes human beings as a part of nature and holds that values – be they religious, ethical, social, or political –have their source in human experience and culture. Humanism thus derives the goals of life from human need and interest rather than from theological or ideological abstractions, and asserts that humanity must take responsibility for its own destiny. (http://americanhumanist.org/Humanism/ Definitions_of_Humanism)

The humanist wants to be free of supernaturalism. The religious counterpart is atheism. The atheist wants to be free of supernaturalism, therefore free from the Word of God and there is no authority structure. In the words of the inspired author of Judges, "In those days there was no king in Israel; everyone did what was right in his own eyes" (Judges 21:25). Humanism is also said to recognize human beings as part of nature and holds that values – religious, ethical, social, or political - have their source in human experience and culture. According to humanism, human experience is the objective standard to interpret religious, ethical, social, and political values.

These ideas are not new. The ancient philosopher Democritus believed in the concept of indivisibility. People still talk about things being indivisible. I thought that way, until the Word of God awakened me and the Holy Spirit convicted me of my error. Indivisibility if taken to its logical conclusion means that the universe is one huge atom. Democritus believed that atoms were indivisible. Now the enlightened thinker knows that atoms are divisible because atoms consist of sub-atomic particles. The atom consists of three parts – the proton, the neutron, and the electron. The enlightened thinker has not thought carefully enough to change the name of his material substance. The word atom comes from the Greek word *atomos* which literally means uncut or undivided. We have not only abandoned the Word of God as the only rule for faith and practice, we have abandoned the right use of words as words.

The people of God must have objective definitions of words. More importantly they must have an objective standard to interpret life. The reason Christians feel the intensity of afflictions, persecution, or trials in this life is they have lost a sense of God's character. The reason they have lost a sense of God's character is the evangelical church devoted the past few generations digging in the Bible looking for moral lessons. We cannot learn how to live until we know whom we are living for. The Psalmist understood the fundamental principles about the nature and character of God, not because of his life experiences, but in spite of them. The Psalmist admitted, "I would have perished in my affliction" except that the Word of God was my delight. If experience is our standard, we are doomed or as the Psalmist would say, "we will perish."

The subjective self-appointed judge of faith and practice will result in an uncritical mythological grossly misunderstood interpretation of reality. To put it another way if we think we can interpret life without the Word of God, life will be in a state of turmoil and confusion. The ever changing compounds of this world must not deceive God's people into thinking that God is a compound. He is not. God is indivisible. God is the ultimate independent authority and He gives His Word to His people so they may believe and understand ultimate authority for the soul. This is the fundamental premise taught in the Word of God.

God cannot mutate. God cannot change, "For I am the Lord, I do not change (Malachi 3:6)." As noble and lofty as the immutability of God sounds, it is often a mere assertion used to describe the character of God. This doctrine as many others in the Bible, is mysterious, but must be believed since it is so clearly taught in Holy Scripture. This doctrine of immutability also extends to the Word of God. "Forever, O Lord, Thy Word is settled in heaven." This shows the immutability of God's Word. We cannot see God, but we can see His Word. We not only admit to the unchangeableness of God's character, we can say that God's Word never changes. His Word is fixed. It is established.

The promises of God will never fail. When God promised to give Abraham a son, though humanly impossible, God kept His promise. When God promised to be with Joshua and give him victories over the enemy, God kept His promise. God will always keep His promises to His people. "Then I will give you shepherds after My own heart, who will feed you on knowledge and understanding" (Jeremiah 3:15). Christ gave pastors and teachers "for the equipping of the saints for the work of ministry" (Ephesians 4:12). The people of God are equipped with the Word of God and all the principles in it. However, the sin nature is in conflict with the Word of God. The unbelieving, unrepentant sinner is opposed to God and His Word. God warns them but they will not listen. For instance, before the fall of Jerusalem in 586 B.C. the Lord spoke through the prophet Jeremiah.

> And the Lord said, "Because they have forsaken My law which I set before them, and have not obeyed My voice, nor walked according to it, but they have walked according to the dictates of their own hearts and after the Baals, which their fathers taught them," therefore thus says the Lord of hosts, the God of Israel: "Behold, I will feed them, this people, with wormwood, and give them water of gall to drink. I will scatter them also among the Gentiles, whom neither they nor their fathers have known. And I will send a sword after them until I have consumed them." (Jeremiah 9:13-16)

All of God's promises are more certain to happen than yesterday. However all of God's promises are not promises of wrath and punishment. Those promises only apply to the children of Satan. For God's children, God's promises an eternal favorable relation with God the Father, God the Son and God the Holy Spirit. "He who believes in the Son has eternal life; but he who does not obey the Son shall not see life, but the wrath of God abides on him" (John 3:36).

Christians find comfort, relief, and peace in the Word of God, even if affliction continues throughout life. Affliction is necessary to wean us from our worldly sinful desires. As the apostle Peter said "for a little while, if need be, you have been grieved by various trials" (1 Peter 1:6). God sends affliction to turn His church from the wickedness of pride and arrogance to the Word of God for the saving of the soul. Not only does the Word of God teach the way of salvation, it teaches Christians how to bear the trials and afflictions of this life. The Word of God ought to be the delight for every Christian. The Word of God ought to be so indelibly fixed in your mind so that you can say like the Psalmist, "I will never forget your precepts." The unchangeable permanency of God's Word is the only remedy you will find for the afflictions of this life. There have been times in the American culture that people used popular phrases like "United We Stand." People that unite by profession to a sinful creed, no matter how noble it may be, will find themselves terribly scattered. The only true unity we will find is under the unchangeable authority of God and His Word. If God's people will be reformed by the Word of God, then they will have made the first step to reform our society so that words become meaningful.

14. Sound Understanding

Oh, how I love Your law! It is my meditation all the day. You, through Your commandments, make me wiser than my enemies; For they are ever with me. I have more understanding than all my teachers, for Your testimonies are my meditation. I understand more than the ancients, because I keep Your precepts. I have restrained my feet from every evil way, that I may keep Your Word. I have not departed from Your judgments, for You Yourself has taught me. How sweet are Your Words to my taste, sweeter than honey to my mouth! Through Your precepts I get understanding; Therefore I hate every false way.

Psalm 119:97-104

The word "love" is virtually impossible to define. It is one of those words most often defined by what it is "like" rather than stating in a clear concise definition the meaning of the word. To show you how the English speaking world has grossly misunderstood the word love, I call your attention to the frequently used romantic expression - "I fell in love." People do not fall in love; they fall in a ditch. You love someone or someone loves you. If love is a condition, an outside force cannot invade it. If love is an action, it could not possibly act upon itself. Love describes, acts upon someone or something, or it has an object. The object of love for the Psalmist was the Word of God.

The 16th century Reformer, Martin Luther, said, "The greater the love, the more like God." He went on to explain: "the more a person loves, the closer he approaches the image of God." Love is an attribute of God, but it is one of many. I conclude that Luther intends "love" to be an expression of affection and a display of selfless service. Jesus came to serve, not to be served. Jesus showed pity to a wayward world. Jesus became obedient to the point of death. Love was something that Jesus did to express that dimension of God's character. Love is something you should do to express the image of God imprinted on your soul.

The Psalmist was a lover of the Word of God with his whole being. The Psalmist said, "I love Your law." "Your law" is a reference to the God's Word, which includes God's law. The language indicates a present active certainty. The Psalmist loved the Word of God all the time. He was engaged with the Word of God. It was ultimate reality that gave the Word of God authority from the ultimate source, the triune God.

Unbelievers may believe some portion of God's Word, but they do not see it as the absolute authority for life and duty. For that reason, the Word of God is disgusting and even repulsive to unbelievers. Unbelievers belong to the family of Satan and believers belong to the family of God. If the unbeliever's heart was not too hardened, the Word of God may be tolerated, but still hated. No! The child of God says, "I love the Word of God." In fact, the child of God should have the same attitude as the Psalmist. There should be an inexpressible love for the Word of God. The Psalmist loved the Word of God to a degree that is unheard of today. The Psalmist meditated on the Word of God all day. He was so full of the Word of God that his thoughts were upon the Word of God during the most difficult time. He thought about the Word of God all day long. During the day the Psalmist kept his mind on the Word of God even though he was busy working, raising a family, making a living, and struggling against the wicked men around him. At night the Psalmist could rest, but during the day his enemies wanted to kill him. The evidence for the love of God is the love of God's Word.

> The cords of the wicked have bound me (Psalm 119:61).

The proud have forged a lie against me (Psalm 119:69).

The proud have dug pits for me (Psalm 119:85).

In the midst of his troubles the Psalmist loved the Word of God and meditated upon it all during the day. The troubles western Christians face in this life, come and go. The Psalmist was not so fortunate. He said, "My enemies are ever with me." It does not mean they were there 24 hours a day, but they were always seeking to destroy him. However, he derived comfort from the Word of God.

It does not matter where you are on the spiritual growth chart. You may be a new Christian, you may be drinking milk or you may be eating spiritual T-bones, but wherever you are on the spiritual growth chart, you need sound understanding from the Word of God. It is the ultimate source for sound understanding and true spiritual wisdom.

The Psalmist makes no bones about his attitude toward what he calls "every false way." Let me put that in language that no one will misunderstand. The Psalmist hates lies and liars, because he had sound understanding and true spiritual wisdom from God's mouth.

"Your commandments make me wiser than my enemies" demonstrates the wisdom of the Psalmist. He realized his enemies were not ignorant. However, possessing knowledge does not insure wisdom. It is possible to have knowledge without wisdom, but you cannot have wisdom without knowledge. The Psalmist does not compare his knowledge with that of his enemies, who are obviously unbelievers, but rather he compares his godly wisdom to the unbeliever's understanding. His enemies were men of human learning. They may have been experts of the natural world, but they did not know the God of nature. If they did not know the God of nature, they certainly did not understand the wisdom of God's commandments. Those same principles apply to Christians in this present age. The goal of wisdom is the life of obedience to God.

> Surely I have taught you statutes and judgments, just as the Lord my God commanded me, that you should act according to them in the land which you go to possess. Therefore be careful to observe them; for this is your wisdom and your understanding in the sight of the peoples who will hear all these statutes, and say, "Surely this great nation *is* a wise and understanding people." (Deuteronomy 4:5-6)

The Psalmist was confident of his sound understanding. "I have more understanding than all my teachers" (Psalm 119:99). The teachers of the covenant community in Israel at that time were the priests and Levites. They should have studied the Law of Moses, because they were in the chair of Moses. However, some of those teachers of Israel neglected the law of God. They were interested in their own honor. They were interested in their own pocket books. They were interested in the tradition and formalities of religion.

Later the prophet Hosea asserted, "there is no truth or mercy or knowledge of God in the land" (Hosea 4:1). Hosea accused the priests of turning their back on the knowledge of God. "My people are destroyed for lack of knowledge. Because you have rejected knowledge, I also will reject you from being priest for Me, because you have forgotten the law of your God..." (Hosea 4:6). Those priests (preachers) had understanding, but it was not sound understanding. Likewise, in the contemporary church many preachers have understanding, but not sound understanding.

The Psalmist had a sound understanding of the Word of God even more than the men of previous generations. This may mean that the Word of God gave the Psalmist a better understanding of the tradition and doctrine that was passed down through the generations. From our youth we are taught to love experience and the voices of the present culture. If we are diligent in our spiritual lives we might try to summarize our faith and review it occasionally. The Word of God is the ultimate rule, but how often do Christians meditate on it the way the Psalmist describes his affection for and dedication to the Word of God?

The Word of God is the instrument God uses to reveal His saving truth. The Word of God is more than just a book that explains the happy ending to the troubles in this life. True biblical wisdom accompanies sound understanding so that according to the Psalmist you will be "wiser than your enemies." When you engage in war, you must be wiser than your enemy lest he prevail against you.

Martin Luther allegedly said that wisdom was the noblest gift that man had. I clarify by saying, "spiritual wisdom." We live in a fallen sinful world. Christians live in the fallen sinful world and as James said, "Christians will fall into various trials." When we face the troubles of this life we must ask God to give us true spiritual wisdom. James says if we ask for wisdom from God it will be given liberally.

When the Old Testament saints rejected the Word of God and eventually adopted false religions of every sort, God punished them by sending them into captivity. God took them from temple worship, scattered them into foreign lands, and they became slaves to the ungodly nations.

When God brought them back to Israel to rebuild the temple, God also gave them the Word of God. "Now on the second day the heads of the fathers' houses of the all the people, with the priests and Levites, were gathered to Ezra the scribe, in order to understand the Words of the Law" (Nehemiah 8:13).

There is an analogy that the church should draw from the Old Testament Israel. Like Israel was in captivity the church is in captivity. The modern church lives in a world that says no to the Word of God and yes to individualism. The church lives in a world that hates the idea that God is sovereign. Living in that environment is like living in captivity, but God gathers His church together like He did the Israelites to give them the Word of God.

If you want to hate the false ways of the world, then you must love the Word of God so you will have sound understanding and true spiritual knowledge.

Study the Word of God.
Inquire into the Word of God.
Search the Word of God.

15. The Center of Life

Your Word is a lamp to my feet and a light to my path. I have sworn and confirmed that I will keep Your righteous judgments. I am afflicted very much; Revive me, O LORD, according to Your Word. Accept, I pray, the freewill offerings of my mouth, O LORD, and teach me Your judgments. My life is continually in my hand, yet I do not forget Your law. The wicked have laid a snare for me, yet I have not strayed from Your precepts. Your testimonies I have taken as a heritage forever, for they are the rejoicing of my heart. I have inclined my heart to perform Your statutes forever, to the very end.

Psalm 119:105-112

The Psalmist suffered as a result of the treacherous evil men in his world. They lied about the Psalmist and tried to do bodily harm to him. Godly men will always suffer at the hand of the evil one. The ungodly man is insensitive toward other rational human beings, because he thinks he is the center of the world. He thinks no one else is important. "I am and there is no one else besides me" was the outrageous claim of the king of Babylon (Isaiah 47:10).

It is alleged that God permits all kinds of evil, insensitive and unloving circumstances to plague His people. It is not uncommon to hear people blame God for the ungodliness of the world. Adam and Eve and everybody since have tried to lay the blame at the feet of someone else. For example, Adam sinned and God confronted Adam, then Adam blamed Eve, and she blamed the snake. No one was ready to take responsibility. The authority of God should have humbled Adam, but like other sinful creatures, Adam had no respect for the authority over him. The same applies today. Who wants to accept the responsibility for the moral degradation in society?

Who wants to accept the responsibility for the unstable anti-intellectual society? No one! Everyone wants to blame the moral problems of society on someone else. Everyone wants to blame our anti-intellectualism on someone else. Generally speaking people tend to interpret the world and everything around them with gross inconsistencies. The consistency of interpretative theory found in intelligent discourse in the postmodern world is about as stable as a jellyfish on a dry beach.

Generally speaking people tend to interpret the world and everything in it based on their own subjective ideas and their own experience in life. Christians tend to approach Scripture with dim eyes at best and sometimes they are blinded because the cultural, social, ideological and philosophical assumptions have colored their understanding of Scripture. More particularly self-conceit resulting from sinful pride colors, if not darkens, the right understanding of the Word of God.

Those people who live in the pride of self-esteem are at least consistent because they tend to think they are the center of the Universe. I remember a missionary telling about being stranded on a mountain road in Brazil. When his jeep engine overheated he was forced to stop in a village for help. It was there that he discovered that the local people thought they lived at the center of the world. Some people are like that today. They not only think they live at the center of the world, they think they are the center of the world. There is a difference between people who think they are the center of the world and those Brazilians who believed they lived at the center of the world. They actually had a tall slender rock to mark the location of the center of the world.

In the postmodern world, there is no mark to locate the center. It happens to be wherever the subject thinks it should be. I wish Christians would stop for a moment and think about the center of all things. The center of all things is not happiness, sports, entertainment, and certainly not religion.

The center of all things is the source of all things and that is God. The Bible plainly teaches that God created all things and had no pre-existing materials for the work of creation. God spoke everything into existence. God said "let there be light." The crowning act of God's creation is found in the words, "let us make man in our image." God is the creator, sustainer, and manager of the universe. Therefore, why would any person professing the Christian religion claim to be the center of all things? The seldom recognized fact is that Christians and all people on earth are absolutely dependent on God who is the source of life. God is the center and heartbeat of the universe. God is independent of creation, yet He is the center of creation.

Sin infects all of creation because the first man violated God's covenant. The only way to enjoy a favorable relation with God is for God to provide the way of salvation and eternal life. Christians believe that God provides all things necessary for faith and life. Are those assertions true? Then why do Christians live as if they are in control? The Psalmist has spoken loud and clear about the condition of the world throughout Psalm 119.

There is an unrelenting effort by the evil one and all his angels to sow evil, wickedness, hatred, and discord among those who profess faith in the Lord Jesus Christ, the one true and living God. Christians ought to say as the Psalmist said, "the wicked have laid a snare for me" (Psalm 119:110). The wicked man thinks he is the center of the world; therefore, his evil is perpetrated by his own self-centeredness. The wicked man could care less about you or anyone else. He is the center of the world.

God is the center of the universe, but God is a Spirit so He communicates His will in His Word so His Word becomes central to life. His Word is the means by which His people can keep a proper perspective in the face of danger, affliction, and persecution. The Word of God is not an idol, but it should be found in the center of our lives. The Psalmist gives a very good reason for having the Word of God as the centerpiece of our lives. The Word of God is a lamp to your feet. This common metaphor explains something about the world. When do you need a lamp? Is it during the daylight or at night? It is during the night. It reminds Christians that they live in a dark world. This is not pessimist thinking, but acknowledges the reality of sin in the world. If you walk into a dark room and light a lamp or a candle, the light becomes the center of all activity. The light will provide the means to show you the way. The light will keep you from stumbling. Darkness represents a wicked world with wicked people seeking our souls for the eternal Hell to which they expect to spend eternity. Christians have the light which represents God's favor and the promises of heaven which is found in the Word of God.

> Vindicate me, O God, and plead my case against an ungodly nation; O deliver me from the deceitful and unjust man! For Thou art the God of my strength; why hast Thou rejected me? Why do I go mourning because of the oppression of the enemy? O send out Thy light and Thy truth, let them lead me; Let them bring me to Thy holy hill, And to Thy dwelling places. Then I will go to the altar of God, To God my exceeding joy; And upon the lyre I shall praise Thee, O God, my God. Why are you in despair, O my soul? And why are you disturbed within me? Hope in God, for I shall again praise Him, The help of my countenance, and my God. (Psalm 43:1-5)

The light from the Word of God will not only give Christians hope in a wicked world, it will show them their sins and duties toward God. The light from the Word of God will prevent them from falling into the darkness. It is with great sadness that so many profess faith in the giver of life and light and yet by their actions turn to death and darkness. Natural man lives in darknes; this is his heritage. He is in bondage to the heritage of darkness.

The new man or woman in Christ has God's special saving grace enabling him or her to choose another heritage. Scripture explains the Christian inheritance. "I have inherited Your testimonies forever, for they are the joy of my heart. I have inclined my heart to perform Your statutes forever, even to the end" (Psalm 119:111-112). To put it another way, the Psalmist declares: "I have taken a heritage." It implies a choice. It means he made it a duty in his life to have an interest in the Word of God. Inheriting the Word of God makes God the center of life with all of His gracious provisions and promises, for this life and the life to come.

16. Hate One, Love the Other

I hate the double-minded, but I love Your law. You are my hiding place and my shield; I hope in Your Word. Depart from me, you evildoers, for I will keep the commandments of my God! Uphold me according to Your Word, that I may live; And do not let me be ashamed of my hope. Hold me up, and I shall be safe, and I shall observe Your statutes continually. You reject all those who stray from Your statutes, for their deceit is falsehood. You put away all the wicked of the earth like dross; Therefore I love Your testimonies. My flesh trembles for fear of You, and I am afraid of Your judgments.

Psalm 119:113-120

This Psalm is best understood by understanding the synonymous characteristics used in this ancient text. There are seven phrases that require special attention throughout Psalm 119. Although I listed these in chapter two, they need to be repeated.

> Your Law
> Your Word
> Your Commandments (of God)
> Your Statutes
> Your Precepts
> Your Testimonies
> Your Judgments

Those seven references express the fullness of the Word of God that was available to the Psalmist. In summary, the Psalmist affirms his love for the Word of God. *Love Is a Many-Splendored Thing*, may be a good title for a movie, but too often *love is a many-splintered thing*. The Word "love" is abstract because of the multiple nuances for the word. Love is a generic term that encompasses rational content as well as emotional expressions. Love for the Word of God is in conflict with the evil in this world. It is sufficient to say the Word of God is the rule of faith and life for Christians. Their faith is an expression of their relationship with God. Their life is an expression of their relationship with other people. Without the Word of God, faith and life become expressions of hopelessness. Unfortunately, many professing Christians have ignored the Word of God. They know little of the content and less of the meaning of God's Word. Exponentially worse is the lack of living according to the Word of God. Too often evangelical Christians come to God's Word with the interpretive eyes of life's experience. They may know the Word of God superficially and they know the clichés and they put on a mask, but privately and sometimes publicly they interpret Scripture based on their sinful feelings. Christians who love the Word of God should not fall prey to the false teachers. If Christians love the Word of God, they must hate anything contrary to the Word of God.

The Word "hate" conjures up all kinds of misunderstanding. However, the Bible leaves no stone unturned. "I hate, I despise your feast days and I do not savor your sacred assemblies" (Amos 5:21). The Lord spoke through the prophet Hosea saying, "All their wickedness is in Gilgal for there I hated them" (Hosea 9:15). Gilgal was the pivotal point of return during Israel's conquest and return to the Promised Land. Gilgal was where the covenant of circumcision was renewed. Gilgal was the place where the Old Testament church celebrated the Passover for the first time since they came out of Egypt. Gilgal was the place the congregation assembled to worship their Redeemer. Gilgal was at one time the picture of the church in its covenant faithfulness and its worship to the true and living God. It was like grapes and figs in the wilderness. Adopting the heathen ways of the surrounding nations, a once fertile church was now fruitless.

God unequivocally condemned their unfaithfulness. New Testament Christians should not dismiss God's Word in the book of Hosea.

> "For there I hated them." Although the place of worship became a place of corrupt and false worship, the sad truth is that God hated the people who worshipped there. The Hebrew verb translated "hate" does not mean what contemporary Christians attach to the meaning of the word hate. Personal emotions are beside the point when the Bible speaks of God's love or his hatred. Love and hate are not exclusively emotional; there is a rational equity about those words. Scripture proves that God never turns His back on His church; it is the church that turns away from God and becomes fruitless. (*Return to the Lord*, by Martin Murphy, p. 91-92)

God's people should expect to obey God, but evidence indicates that many professing Christians have no interest in obedience. However, for those who do want to obey God, they must hate evil. If you love evil you are not a friend of God. When Ahab called the prophets to meet on Mt. Carmel, Elijah realized that he stood alone. Scripture explains what it means to stand faithful with the Word of God.

> And Elijah came near to all the people and said, "How long will you hesitate between two opinions? If the Lord is God, follow Him; but if Baal, follow him." But the people did not answer him a Word. Then Elijah said to the people, "I alone am left a prophet of the Lord, but Baal's prophets are four hundred and fifty men." (1 Kings 18:21-22)

Hating evil was not popular in the days of Elijah and it is not popular in our day. What can a principled man do living in the wickedness of this world?

First, he can hate evil doers.
Second, he can love the Word of God.
Third, he can obey the Word of God.

If we believe the Word of God is inspired and true then we should tell evil-minded people where to go. "Depart from me evildoers" (Psalm 119:115). Godly principled Christians should hold evildoers in disdain because "their deceit is falsehood."

Deceitfulness is a sin established by the ninth commandment and confirmed in the full counsel of God. You shall not bear false witness against your neighbor. Liars are often mentioned by the Lord and His apostles and for a very good reason. A lie is opposite of the truth and God is truth. Therefore, the ultimate standard for truth is the mind of God. To be opposed to truth is to be opposed to God and all of His excellences. If Christians love the Word of God, they love the truth. For instance, if we are consistent and faithful in our thinking there is only one true gospel. Yet there are three gospels being preached by Protestant Christians.

1. Social gospel
2. Man-centered gospel
3. God-centered gospel

There are many miscellaneous gospels. Not only is there a singular gospel, there is singular moral truth. Private moral judgments do not count unless they line up with the Word of God. Moral truth is rooted in the integrity, trustworthiness, and faithfulness of God. Therefore, moral truth is an attribute of God. Holy Scripture commands obedience of God's moral law and truth is of the essence of God's moral law, therefore it is a duty to love moral truth. In Romans chapter one Paul explained how an unregenerate human race had exchanged the truth of God for a lie (Romans 1:25). The unbelieving human mind is filled with lies until the Holy Spirit of God changes the mind to understand and believe the truth in the Word of God.

Some Christian leaders believe liars are more abundant today than ever before, therefore suggesting there are fewer believers today than ever before. Liars have always been in great abundance. God's people were about to fall into the hands of the great King Nebuchadnezzar and the Lord prophesied through the prophet Jeremiah about the abundance of liars. He stated that truth had perished and had been cut off from their mouth. The prophets (false) held fast to deceit. The false pen of the scribe certainly worked falsehood and everyone was dealing falsely. Read Jeremiah chapters seven and eight for a thorough report.

Those words remind me of the church of our day. All fraud and hypocrisy is hateful to God. Hypocrisy is pretending to be truly religious, but hypocritical religion is an outward religion. As unpopular as it may be, Christians must hate the haters of God by challenging their false gospel, their evil confessions and their evil behavior.

Christians who violate the ninth commandment will find refuge in the righteousness of the one who is the Truth, the Lord Jesus Christ. Those who turn to Christ will find the truth. The church will love to keep the truth. God's people must say as the Psalmist said, "I hate those who are double minded."

When we see the danger of being enemies of God,
then we can be humbled by His Word,
then we can show Him respect,
then we can show Him reverence,

then we can show the proper love and be loved because of the saving grace of the Lord Jesus Christ.

God's people must say, "I love the Word of God."

17. Servant in a Sinful World

I have done justice and righteousness; Do not leave me to my oppressors. Be surety for Your servant for good; Do not let the proud oppress me. My eyes fail from seeking Your salvation and Your righteous Word. Deal with Your servant according to Your mercy, and teach me Your statutes. I am Your servant; Give me understanding, that I may know Your testimonies. It is time for You to act, O Lord, for they have regarded Your law as void. Therefore I love Your commandments more than gold, yes, than fine gold! Therefore all Your precepts concerning all things I consider to be right; I hate every false way.

Psalm 119:121-128

This portion of Psalm 119 like every other octonary in Psalm 119 is as fresh as today's newspaper. The Psalmist was a man engaged in his culture. However, he was not married to his culture. The man of God was standing in opposition to the culture of his day. Godly men and women have always found opposition and persecution in an ungodly culture. God's people are always at odds with sinful culture. There is no utopia. The transcendentalist of the 19th century failed in their attempt to form a perfect community. We are not living in the new heavens and the new earth. The liberal theologians have craftily persuaded their followers that man is basically good.

The same old lie was preached by the pelagians in the 5th century and the socinians of the 16th century. The Pelagian false teaching emerged in 5th century under the teaching of a professing Christian named Pelagius. He taught that man was born innocent, but by his own choice and power he sinned against God. He also believed that unredeemed man could do good thus man's own effort is necessary for salvation apart from God's special grace. Socinus of the16[th] century did not believe that the death of Christ on the cross was necessary for salvation, because God could forgive sins without the atonement of Jesus Christ. Today the name of that false teaching is "liberalism." It is wicked crafty people who infiltrate the church with the express purpose of choking God to death. Those crafty ungodly people wear pretty dresses and nice suits. They smile and sing the songs. Some of them even recite the statement of faith. Some of them teach Sunday School. However, deep down inside they are Pelagian at heart. Many of them do not believe there is anything after this life. If those who have departed this life could talk to you today they would tell you to be prepared because death does not bring an end to existence. In fact, it is just the beginning. However, for the ones who do believe that man is appointed once to die and then the judgment, Psalm 119 is a wake-up call.

The Word of God in this Psalm describes, in the most graphic terms, the wickedness of this world. It talks about the wicked men who persecute godly men. It talks about the proud ungodly man seeking to destroy the godly man. It talks about the double-minded men as the evildoers in this world. These ungodly men are oppressors. The wisdom writer explains:

> Then I returned and considered all the oppression that is done under the sun. And look! The tears of the oppressed, but they have no comforter - on the side of their oppressors there is power, but they have no comforter. (Ecclesiastes 4:1)

Power hungry people are naturally oppressors. People are not basically good. They are basically bad. It is the basic badness that makes them do oppressive things. They want to control other people. They want to tyrannize other people.

The tyranny of the cultural elite is the agenda for the postmodern culture. The cultural elite believe they know what is best for everyone else. The tyranny of political liberalism is rampant in public life. The tyranny of social engineering is undermining the once strong civic institutions in America.

One man wants to be a tyrant over another because of a bad heart that has bad motives. In every walk of life and in every institution there are oppressors. They are in government. They are business men. They attend church meetings. The Psalmist lived among oppressors and we have them among us and they will remain until the end of the world.

Living among the wicked oppressive sinners requires endurance and spiritual strength from upon high. Professing Christians who live like wicked oppressors do not reflect the biblical view; They should hate every false way and love the truth. There is another way for God's children. It is the way of justice and righteousness. The Psalmist said, "I have done justice and righteousness." This does not refer to perfectionism. The Psalmist was not like the pietist of our day. A pietist is one who believes from his own subjective experience that he is in a right relationship with God. Scripture is used merely to give that inward subjective religion some credibility to the public.

Justice and righteousness is an action of the Psalmist, not a condition of the Psalmist. By doing justice and righteousness he is simply deciding between right and wrong based on an objective standard. To put it another way, the Word of God was his measuring stick. The Word of God distinguishes whether or not something is right or wrong. It is unbecoming of a Christian to fail in his or her responsibility to do justice and righteousness. The new creature in Christ will show his faith by his works. His works are of the nature described in the Bible. His works are not subjective products of the pietistic gauntlet. When the church allows its members to oppress others, the witness of the church is seriously crippled.

Oppressive tyrants are incapable of doing justice and righteousness. Oppression and injustice should not be allowed in the church and in the case of a healthy biblical church, oppression and injustice is not permitted. In the case of an individual Christian, pleading the case before God in private prayer like the Psalmist did in Psalm 119 is in order. The Psalmist prayed, "Do not let the proud oppress me." The Psalmist had his eyes set on the Lord's salvation so the Psalmist prayed for the Lord's mercy.

The Psalmist understood his relationship to the Lord as a servant (Psalm 119:125). The relationship of the servant to the master is one of submission and dedication. A good servant will avoid oppression because he will submit to His master. If God's people submit to the Lord and dedicate themselves to His Word, there would never be oppression from the church. A servant of the Lord will recognize his servant position. The servant will surely fail to serve with perfection. However, his defects and his shortcomings will not exclude him from being a servant of God. The Master will show mercy to his servant. However, an honorable servant may be tempted to say, "but I want to see the oppressor get his due." The Lord responds to the servant, "vengeance is mine says the Lord." In due time, the oppressor will get his due from the hand of the Lord.

Great and full is the joy of those who serve a master of forgiveness, redemption, and mercy. Who will you choose to be your master? One who brings sorrow and misery or one who gives the sweetness of grace and mercy? One who keeps you in sinful bondage or one who gives full liberty? Good servants will always choose the way of mercy, grace and liberty. If that is true then why is there so much tyranny and oppression? I believe the answer can be found in the lack of interest in theology. Since theology is the study of God, the place to learn about Him is the Word of God. Christians do not understand God because they do not understand His Word. If Christians do not know the Word of God, then they cannot know how to be good servants. Let me give you one example of how some professing Christians misunderstand the Word of

God. "Deal with Your servant according to Your mercy, and teach me Your statutes." Does the Psalmist mean mercy in salvation or mercy in moral behavior? There are two biblical principles in this regard.

In salvation God deals to His people according to justice. In morals God deals with His people according to mercy.

After God saves His people he is certainly merciful because of His goodness. Christians must have the mind of God to know how to live sanely and Christly. It is for that reason the Psalmist said: "I love your commandments" – the Word of God. The Word of God is more important than gold even the best gold pales in importance to the eternal Word of the living God. If the living Word is your life, then let the written Word be your love.

18. Passionate Christian

Your testimonies are wonderful; Therefore my soul keeps them. The entrance of Your Words gives light; It gives understanding to the simple. I opened my mouth and panted, For I longed for Your commandments. Look upon me and be merciful to me, as Your custom is toward those who love Your name. Direct my steps by Your Word, and let no iniquity have dominion over me. Redeem me from the oppression of man, that I may keep Your precepts. Make Your face shine upon Your servant, and teach me Your statutes. Rivers of water run down from my eyes, because men do not keep Your law.
Psalm 119:129-136

The one feature in Psalm 119, the main feature in fact, is that the Bible is the Word of God, composed, written, and designed for the believer. The believer is under the special care of God and it is for that reason that God gives the believer the great body of wisdom, counsel, injunction, and excellency found in the Word of God. The Word of God reveals the wisdom to know God and to know his plan for the Christian life. It gives counsel to know God's holiness and injunctions or commands to keep Christians from turning to false gods. It is the ultimate authority for Christians to learn and understand the excellences of God's nature and character.

Many professing Christians reduce the Bible to a super-natural "how to" book revealing all the secrets for a successful life. The Bible does tell us how to live, but first we must know the source of life. The Bible reveals the essence, nature, and character of the triune God. It appears that we live in a time when people care less what God is like. There are only a few who are willing to devote the detailed time and scrupulous investigation into the Word of God in order to learn who God is. The unbeliever's knowledge of God and the believer's knowledge of God are radically different. Paul explains the root of the problem.

> For since the creation of the world His invisible attributes are clearly seen, being understood by the things that are made, even His eternal power and Godhead, so that they are without excuse, because, although they knew God, they did not glorify Him as God, nor were thankful, but became futile in their thoughts, and their foolish hearts were darkened. (Romans 1:20-21)

The Bible not only tells us about God, it expresses the divine purpose of God. It should please God's people to learn God's purpose so that they might glorify God apart from their self-interest. Many professing Christians are passionate about hearing a Word from the Lord. However, there are professing Christians looking for a new word from the Lord. There may be several reasons that they seek some new word, thus new knowledge of God. Many professing Christians are not willing to do the necessary work to gain knowledge of God from the Scriptures. They prefer the way of *fideism*.

> The Latin Word *fide* literally translated "faith" and the English "ism" is a noun forming suffix often associated with a world view. It means to believe something by faith without any rational evidence. There is an old maxim attributed to St. Hilary of the 5th century worth remembering. "A person cannot express what he does not know and he cannot believe what he cannot express." *Fideism* will produce theological disaster because it has no metaphysical basis. (*Theological Terms in Layman Language*, by Martin Murphy, p. 44.)

The first purpose of Scripture is to teach Christians the nature and character of the triune God. The second purpose of Scripture is to teach the triune God is absolutely sovereign. Open Holy Scripture and look for God rather than your own preconceived notions. If Christians seek Him they will find Him on every page. To know God, Christians must have a passion for God. Christians must distinguish between ungodly passions and godly passions.

For example, in 1 Thessalonians 4:3 the Bible clarifies this doctrine. "For this is the will of God, your sanctification; that you should abstain from sexual immorality; that each of you should know how to possess his own vessel in sanctification and honor; not in passion of lust like the Gentiles who do not know God." The word "passion" and the word "sex" have almost become interchangeable in recent history. Part of the fault lies with the modernist view of relativity, part of it lies with the postmodern deconstructionist, but I think for the most part the anti-intellectual agenda has twisted the proper use of words. Actually the English Word "passion" comes from the Latin Word *passio* which literally means "to suffer." For instance the suffering of Christ on the cross is spoken of as the passion of Christ.

The Old Testament describes passions in a variety of ways. The book of Proverbs explains the danger of passions. "A tranquil heart is life to the body, but passion is rottenness to the bones" (Proverbs 14:30). So there is a sinful passion which leads to a variety of outward actions that are unbecoming of the Christian. The Word "passion" translated from the Hebrew is the same word that is translated into English as "zeal." Another familiar Bible verse that uses the word "zeal" is found in Isaiah.

> Of the increase of His government and peace there will be no end, upon the throne of David and over His kingdom, to order it and establish it with judgment and

> justice from that time forward, even forever. The zeal
> of the Lord of hosts will perform this. (Isaiah 9:7)

So God's passion is holy and good. To put it another way, there are good passions and bad passions. There are vast differences between the passionate unbeliever and the passionate Christian. The passionate unbeliever is self-centered, self-indulgent, and self-seeking. The passionate Christian is God-centered, devoted to the labor of love, and desires to have an interest in Jesus Christ.

The church, hyperbolically speaking, has lost a zeal for God, God's purposes, and God's providential expressions. Some professing Christians have little passion for the Word of God. The Psalmist, a man inspired by God, shows his passion for the Word of God and how the Word of God has changed his life. He expressed his passion for the Word of God in a voice of excitement. "Your [God's] testimonies are wonderful" (Psalm 119:129). The word "testimony" is a legal term that has been used throughout history to refer to a "witness." A sworn witness is one who tells exactly what he or she has seen or heard under oath. Christians must understand the Word of God to be a witness for it. They must understand that God is Spirit and then witness the truth of it. They must understand that God is infinite, all-powerful, everywhere present, and knows everything. Knowing, believing, and understanding are not enough. They must be witnesses of the truth in God's Word.

A passion for God and His ways is necessary to find ful-fillment in the Christian life. The Psalmist expresses his passion for God by commanding God to intervene in the life of the Psalmist. The Psalmist said, "Direct my steps by your Word." The passionate Christian has the Holy Spirit driving him or her toward a deep affection for the Word of God.

Christians have the large body of divine direction; It is the Bible. It is the duty of every Christian to pray for God's grace so their lives will be regulated by the Word of God. Christians ought to have the passion to pray asking God, "let no iniquity have dominion over me." A passionate Christian will not be very popular because he or she will have the zeal to love God and hate evil. The Word of God and the Holy Spirit are the means by which Christians will love God and hate evil. Passionate Christians will love God and understand their utter dependency on God. Passions are good, but they must be under the direction of the Spirit of God according to His Word. It is a sad theater to watch the lives of professing Christians who have no regard for the Word of God. The passionate unbeliever has a passion for pleasure, happiness, material satisfaction and independence from God.

The Passionate Christian loves the Word of God because it shows the way to eternal life. Then a stream of tears will be appropriate for the passionate Christian seeking to walk with God according to God's regulative principle.

19. Whose Justice? Which Life?

Righteous are You, O Lord, and upright are Your judgments. Your testimonies, which You have commanded, are righteous and very faithful. My zeal has consumed me, because my enemies have forgotten Your Words. Your Word is very pure; Therefore Your servant loves it. I am small and despised, yet I do not forget Your precepts. Your righteousness is an everlasting righteousness, and Your law is truth. Trouble and anguish have overtaken me, yet Your commandments are my delights. The righteousness of Your testimonies is everlasting; Give me understanding, and I shall live.

Psalm 119:137-144

Ultimate authority requires ultimate perfection which is the nature of God. "Your [God's] testimonies...are righteous and very faithful." If God is perfectly righteous, then His Word is perfectly righteous. The righteousness of God is seldom disputed in theological debates among professing Christians. But the righteousness of God is sorely despised in practical concerns of life. The righteous God is honest in all His judgments. However, post-fall sinful man is not honest in all his judgments. The modern world slandered honesty and integrity with its hypothetical relativistic announcements. Furthermore, the postmodern culture annihilated honesty and integrity with its interpretative methodology. It is the unrighteous nature of sinful man that causes dishonesty in his judgments.

The word that describes God's righteous judgments is "justice." God's character is such that when we think of His righteousness we think of His justice. Righteousness and justice are often used in the Bible to signify the same idea or concept. It is the concept called justice that is not common to man after the fall. Justice is not common to man because justice is the manifestation of God's holiness.

God commands his people to pursue justice. "You shall follow what is altogether just that you may live and inherit the land which the Lord your God is giving you" (Deuteronomy 16:20). If asked to explain the concept known as "justice," some people might say is it the due process of law. It is true that you cannot have justice without law, but the question is which law is just?

Some people believe justice means that everyone gets the same fair treatment. It is true that you cannot have justice without fair treatment, but the question is: where can you find fair treatment? Yet others might give an analogy such as justice is the result of a judge's decision. It is true that you cannot have justice without a judge, but the judge must be righteous.

Prior to the twentieth century, theologians inquired and wrote voluminously about justice. Today justice is primarily used by the unbelieving world especially when referring to civil or criminal litigation. The term "justice" used in the secular sense is problematic for Christians. How can there be justice in a sinful world? So when we talk about justice, we must ask whose justice? Contemporary moral philosophers like Alasdair McIntyre have tossed around ideas that are largely ignored by the average person. In fact, the few thousand academicians that have read McIntyre are probably left in the dark with his innovative and scholarly pursuits. McIntyre's monumental work entitled *After Virtue* is a complex thesis statement about the concept of justice. Later he wrote *Whose Justice? Which Rationality?* He basically asked the question: "Is there a rational basis for the concept of justice in the postmodern world?" He vigorously argues yes.

Social engineers believe they have the answer to the complex question "whose justice." They proudly boast of uniform standards often referred to as "equal protection under

the law" and "equal justice for all." Everyone agrees that
God's justice will ultimately prevail, but defining justice
becomes obscure in the search. Benjamin Disraeli once said,
"justice is truth in action." Although I'm no fan of Disraeli's
double-edged political career, he could not have spoken
anything more profound or expedient than he did when he said
"justice is truth in action." The legal and moral philosophers of
our age are eager to prove the truth, but the concept of justice
will not stand the test of a sinful mind. McIntyre saw a
connection between rationality and justice positing, "no one
can be practically rational who is not just." God's justice must
and will ultimately prevail because God is truth and can
pronounce nothing but truth, and because He is perfectly
rational. Reinhold Niebuhr argued for justice against the
tyranny of Hitler. He, like Alasdair McIntyre, did not believe
that justice could be administered without the assistance of a
democratic or republican tradition. However, it is not until you
have a proper conception of justice and an objective and
absolute understanding of law that you can say a judgment is
one of a kind. Both men claim to be Christians, yet neither of
them laid a foundation that was everlasting. The justice of God
is everlasting and only His Word is the source of
understanding the justice of God.

     After a careful consideration of the concept of justice it is
safe to say that the Psalmist understood God's justice. We too
should endeavor to understand justice because even though it
is an attribute of God, He has given His people an objective
standard in order to do justice. Conceptual notions of justice
in this sinful world will sometimes lead to confusion and
disbelief.

     The doctrine of God's justice will cause rational creatures
to see themselves for what they are: "I am small and despised,
yet I do not forget your precepts." His humility is not a false
humility. When we see our fragile condition, we have to look
beyond ourselves for objectivity and security. When the

Psalmist saw himself for what he was, he had a good reason to remember the Word of God. Sinful people living in a sinful world will find life difficult at best. The recognition of reality for the unbelieving sinner should bring confession; Then he or she can say, "I am small and despised, yet I do not forget your precepts." The godly ruler stands in direct contradistinction from the tyrannical ruler. The difference between the godly ruler and the tyrant is the deciding mark in every society of people. The godly ruler will be distinguished by the exercise of justice because his judgments are based on truth.

God's justice is perfect, therefore His judgments are perfect. Applied to life, God will not punish or condemn an innocent creature. On the other hand God will punish the guilty. For instance, you think you are innocent and God punishes you; therefore, God must not be righteous in His justice. However, no person is innocent. "For all have sinned and are continually falling short of the glory of God" (Romans 3:23). Sin is the breeding ground for injustice. The wisdom writer in Ecclesiastes also speaks to the injustice he saw in the world: "And look! The tears of the oppressed, but they have no comforter. On the side of the oppressors there is power, but they have no comforter" (Ecclesiastes 4:1). The only relief the oppressed child of God may expect is from God's justice. The children of God go to God for justice because God is righteous.

The oppressed child of God will find relief in God's justice, because of the full and finished atoning work of the Lord Jesus Christ. The unbelievers of this world expect justice, social justice they call it in this secular world, without even knowing what they want. Social Justice is the name given to the human bar of judgment. Social justice demands that Christians do good to all men and abstain from all wrong, fraud, and violence.

The Psalmist declared that the righteousness or the justice of God's Word is everlasting. Then the Psalmist prayed saying, "Give me understanding and I shall live." God's justice secures and guarantees your eternal home with Him. God did not prejudice His justice by forgiving our sins, but in fact made Jesus Christ who knew no sin to be sin on our behalf that we might become the righteousness of God in Him (2 Corinthians 5:21).

20. Divine Proximity

I cry out with my whole heart; Hear me, O Lord! I will keep
Your statutes. I cry out to You; Save me, and I will keep Your
testimonies. I rise before the dawning of the morning, and cry
for help; I hope in Your Word. My eyes are awake through the
night watches, that I may meditate on Your Word. Hear my
voice according to Your lovingkindness; O Lord, revive me
according to Your justice. They draw near who follow after
wickedness; They are far from Your law. You are near, O
Lord, and all Your commandments are truth. Concerning Your
testimonies, I have known of old that You have founded them
forever.

Psalm 119:145-152

The Middle Ages represented a time of superstition and
turbulence in Europe. The culture tortured the people of God.
The American culture entering into the 21st century has a
prevailing influence over the professing evangelical church,
rather than the church having a prevailing influence over the
culture. The church seems to have forgotten its purpose,
mission, and ministry.

The American Culture is not defined by personal
preference, although it may be identified by a psychology of
pessimism or a postmodern psychological delusion. A brief
study of Ancient Near Eastern history and the subsequent
development of western civilization have a common thread
that interweaves every culture on this planet. The common
thread I have in mind is sin. Sin is the father of naturalism.
The naturalistic concept found in modernity and
postmodernity is a major factor found in world and life views
such as individualism, hedonism, relativism, secularism, and
many other anti-Christian philosophies that prevail in many

cultures. The challenge Christians face today has not changed much through the centuries, because western culture identifies itself with anti-Christian thought like it has since the first century. When naturalism captures the heart of a culture one tends to believe that individualism is the solution to challenges such as international crime, political intrigue, economic phantoms and social dishonor. Although God is near the culture, the culture is far away from God.

Individualism is the world and life view that says the individual has a right to do whatever is personally acceptable to that individual. The classic expression of individualism is, "what's good for me is what's good for the rest of the world." Individualism is a high sounding word for plain old selfishness. The worship of self is pure autonomy. The word autonomy means an individual is a law to himself or herself. Autonomous individualism taken to its logical end would mean that a person makes his or her own rules and laws without any objective standard.

Pietistic individualism taken to its logical end leaves the church with no orthodox opinion on anything. For many Christians the popular belief is that the only absolute is that there are no absolutes. So individualism is finally crowned king of the culture.

God looks at His people in community. They are redeemed as individuals, but they are also redeemed as God's covenant people collectively. The individual Christian does not disappear into the collective mass of Christianity. The individual professing Christian is a member of a larger community of Christians known as the visible church.

Individualism has produced a major theological impasse in this country among professing evangelicals. Most of them are unaware of the danger, but it is still present. They talk about indivisibility with little thought or concern for the biblical doctrine on the subject. They even make public vows to indivisibility. Confusing the collective with the individual has brought the church to a very low estate. Pietistic individual personal religion and forgotten biblical doctrine has created a weak, but still alive visible church. Christians should learn from the Psalmist that individualism is the sinful side of Christian thought.

The Psalmist talks in terms of persecution, affliction, oppression, trouble and anguish in his personal life. These are the same kinds of circumstances that every Christian will face from time to time. Sometimes the persecution, affliction, oppression, trouble and anguish is powerfully present and at other times less obvious. When trouble comes your way, individualism is not merely a detriment, it is your destruction. Individualism leaves no room for God. Individualism demands that a person save himself or herself by his or her own efforts or character. So when trouble comes, individualism is no place to turn for help. Individualism and Christianity cannot and never will meet.

When trouble comes your way, divine proximity is the promise and hope for comfort and peace. To paraphrase what the Psalmist says, wicked men dig holes for you to fall in and they persecute you wrongly. Individualism offers no hope, but the promise of Jesus Christ is that He remains with you forever, through thick and thin. Although the Psalmist did not live to see the full and finished work of the Lord Jesus Christ as the redeemer of his elect, the Psalmist asserted with full confidence the promise of divine presence because of the Redeemer.

When you feel the persecution, trouble and anguish of the cultural wickedness, divine proximity will be of great comfort. "They draw near who follow after wickedness; They are far from Your law. You are near, O Lord, and all Your commandments are truth" (Psalm 119:150-151). The enemy is always at hand. The enemy is always near. The enemy is sneaky, cunning, and deceitful in every way, so beware because the enemy is near. The enemy is near, but the enemy can and eventually will be removed. God is near now and forever. Scripture teaches the omnipresence of God. God is everywhere at once. Omnipresence is a fundamental doctrine of the Christian religion. God is present with all things by His power, knowledge and essence. There is no place that escapes the presence of God. The Word of God declares, "God fills heaven and earth" (Jeremiah 23:24). The Psalmist gives a fuller explanation of God's presence.

> Where can I go from Your Spirit? Or where can I flee from Your presence? If I ascend into heaven, You are there; If I make my bed in hell, behold, You are there." (Psalm 139:7-8)

The wicked people of this earth and in the life to come cannot escape the presence and thought of God? The Puritan preacher, Thomas Manton said, "The wicked may run away from God as a friend, but they cannot escape from him as an enemy. Men may try to shut God out of their hearts; and yet he is there, do what they can, and will be found there one day, in the dreadful effects of his anger."

The children of God are not the enemies of God. The children of God love Him and look to Him for comfort and peace. They understand that God is the ultimate and final authority in this life and the life to come. He has given them the Word of God as the ultimate authority for faith and practice. The ultimate authority is living and written and both are near to the child of God.

> The eyes of the Lord are on the righteous, and His ears are open to their cry. The face of the Lord is against those who do evil, to cut off the remembrance of them from the earth. The righteous cry out, and the Lord hears, and delivers them out of all their troubles. The Lord is near to those who have a broken heart, and

saves such as have a contrite spirit. Many are the afflictions of the righteous, but the Lord delivers him out of them all. He guards all his bones; Not one of them is broken. Evil shall slay the wicked, and those who hate the righteous shall be condemned. The Lord redeems the soul of His servants, and none of those who trust in Him shall be condemned. (Psalm 34:15-22)

Divine proximity must not be ignored.

God is near us in His providential care.
God is near us in His Word.
God is near us in His ordinances and sacraments.
God is near His people because Jesus Christ has reconciled His people to Himself.

God is the source of life and comfort. Modernity with all its scientific facts cannot answer questions relative to the source and meaning of life. Now we live in the postmodern world, a world seeking the answers to the complicated questions of life by means of individual psychoanalysis. It is properly called individualism. Has science and psychology given us the answers we search for and need? The answer is no, the pain and hurt remains. People still do not get along with each other. People still feel insecure and restless. We have to go beyond the world of science and psychology to find peace and joy. We are no greater, we are not smarter, and certainly we are not more capable than the man who wrote Psalm 119. He trusted the ultimate authority for the soul.

The normal teaching of Scripture tells us to go beyond ourselves in our search for peace and joy. We must plead for God's lovingkindness. We must plead for God to renew our souls. The Psalmist said, "revive me according to Your justice." The Word "revive" or "renew" means to give new life. It is the restitution of happiness. God must renew the soul and increase the vigor of spiritual life. You will know that God has given you this new life when you become aware that God's Word is the ultimate authority for your soul. Since you belong to Jesus Christ, you have the merit of Christ to cry out and to ask God to hear you in your day of turmoil, struggle and strife.

21. Spiritual Maturity

Consider my affliction and deliver me, for I do not forget Your law. Plead my cause and redeem me; Revive me according to Your Word. Salvation is far from the wicked, for they do not seek Your statutes. Great are Your tender mercies, O Lord; Revive me according to Your judgments. Many are my persecutors and my enemies, yet I do not turn from Your testimonies. I see the treacherous, and am disgusted, because they do not keep Your Word. Consider how I love Your precepts; Revive me, O Lord, according to Your lovingkindness. The entirety of Your Word is truth, and every one of Your righteous judgments endures forever.

Psalm 119:153-160

The term used to describe the life of the Christian in this world is "pilgrim." Christians are often called pilgrims, both in the Bible and the history of the church. They are pilgrims because they realize the temporal nature of life on earth. Christians are steadily moving toward a heavenly city, not built by human hands or made out of wood and stone. They are moving toward a city which has foundations, whose architect and builder is God. The glorious nature of that heavenly city is grossly distorted by all kinds of imaginations of this earthly city. Unfortunately, many preachers and teachers of the Bible do not accurately describe the trip to that glorious city.

A large portion of the evangelical church teaches the pilgrim life in terms of health, wealth, and carnal happiness. The early Reformers like Luther and Calvin, the Puritans, and most Reformed Christians during 19th century understood the nature of the trip to that glorious city. They all understood the pilgrim life was not one of health, wealth, and carnal happiness. They understood the correct nature of the trip, because they understood the ultimate authority for the soul, the Word of God. Without the full counsel of God you will get a distorted view of reality.

Christians are on a trip to the heavenly city while unbelievers are on a trip to the city of torment and pain. Pilgrims try to make sense of the road they travel. It seems as if some of the anti-God travellers fare so well in this life, while godly Christian pilgrims suffer all along the way. It seems that God treats the ungodly so well in this life, but the godly believers have so much trouble. Life in this earthly city is bumpy and sometimes downright treacherous for devout Christians. The Bible often speaks of God's people being afflicted. When God's people were enslaved in Egypt the Lord said, "I have surely seen the affliction of My people who are in Egypt, and have given heed to their cry because of their taskmasters, for I am aware of their sufferings"(Exodus 3:7).

Strange as it may seem, perhaps even paradoxical, God sends affliction as a means of spiritual maturity for the Christian. If you expect your children to mature into responsible productive adults, they must be corrected. Discipline according to an objective standard is absolutely necessary for sound development. It is absolutely necessary that God discipline his children, so they will be ready to set up residence in the heavenly city.

Christians will experience trials and troubles as they travel toward that heavenly city. Paul's "thorn in the flesh" was apparently a physical malady which he interpreted as due to an "angel of Satan in order that he (or "it") might buffet me" (2 Corinthians 12:7). Perhaps he meant the affliction itself was a messenger (rather than an angel), but in any case Satan or one of his demonic angels was responsible. Yet in spite of this Satanic agency Paul knew the affliction was by Divine permission and ultimately for his own good—just as with Job. Job was a man of God afflicted beyond human imagination.

The Bible describes him as a man of great wealth and honor in his society. The Bible describes Job as, "the greatest of all men in the east" (Job 1:3). However, Job lost all his earthly possessions, his sons, and malicious bandits killed his daughters. Then Job suffered physically to the point that his own wife could not tolerate him. It even came to the point that his wife told Job to "curse God and die" (Job 2:9)!

A person's ability to endure affliction is the test of true spiritual maturity. If God afflicted you with a state of poverty, how would you respond? A Christian should respond to providential poverty with this in mind: "The Lord giveth and the Lord taketh away." Nevertheless the Lord is still sovereign and the creature is still dependent on the independent God. A Christian should respond to public harassment for the sake of the gospel by realizing that persecution for the sake of the gospel was a biblical promise. Christians should not be surprised when they take a public stand for truth because they will be castigated by the followers of humanism, relativism, and hedonism or some other temporary world and life view. Disease might be their plight in this life, but in the resurrection body there is no pain or sorrow. There are Christians who live a life of adversity, but God is aware that the adversity is suited to his or her particular needs.

Too often we are like the Psalmist when affliction is our plight. "Why dost Thou hide Thy face, and forget our affliction and our oppression?"(Psalm 44:24). The question is a good question if the right motive is in mind. It is a bad question if the motive is wrong. Christian believers are not entitled to question God's authority, even during affliction. Are Christians entitled to wonder why God does not answer them in their time of need? They may choose to call on God in the same manner the Psalmist called on God in Psalm 119:153: "Consider my affliction and deliver me for I do not forget Your law." God not only reveals Himself in great abundance to His children, he demonstrates it powerfully by the work of the Holy Spirit. Without the Spirit of God, the Bible is nothing more than an academic source of misplaced moralism. "This is my comfort in my affliction, for Your Word has given me life" (Psalm 119:50). Affliction is certain to come your way if you try to please God in this sinful world. Jesus warned his disciples of coming persecutions, to prepare them to endure afflictions with patience, so their hearts would be ready for God's most sufficient grace. This promise of the Lord, predicated upon his pronouncement, "My grace is sufficient for you," is the vantage-point from which you will set your course on the proper biblical perspective. Paul was well content with weaknesses, not because they are desirable in and of themselves, but because they were the means through which God demonstrates his sovereignty, grace, mercy and love.

Doubt, anxiety, affliction and persecution may come your way, but the Word of God instructs Christians to trust Jesus Christ. He has already suffered for the children of God. Salvation is near the child of God, but it is far from the wicked, because the wicked do not hunger and thirst for the Word of God. A deep yearning and desire to know the Lord and His saving grace only comes if you have a deep desire to know the Word of God. His Word will reveal the truth of His saving grace through the Lord Jesus Christ. Christians have the privilege of taking up the cross and cheerfully bearing burdens and afflictions that come into a person's life in the providence of God.

Revival cannot be separated from affliction. It is when affliction comes that Christians must seek revival. The Psalmist repeated his call for personal revival.

Revive me according to Your Word.
Revive me according to Your judgments.
Revive me, according to Your lovingkindness.

Unfortunately, Revivalism from the middle of the 19th century until this very day is the public demonstration of pietism, wrapped in the garbs of biblical renewal. That kind of revival is not equal to spiritual maturity. That type of revivalism is the work of men, not God. True revival is the result of God's work in the individual as well as the entire community of God's people.

The whole counsel of God is your weapon against affliction while you are on your way to spiritual maturity. The whole counsel of God is also the means by which you will come to understand and seek revival. The whole counsel of God is the way to your spiritual maturity.

22. Great Peace From God's Word

Princes persecute me without a cause, but my heart stands in awe of Your Word. I rejoice at Your Word as one who finds great treasure. I hate and abhor lying, but I love Your law. Seven times a day I praise You, because of Your righteous judgments. Great peace have those who love Your law, and nothing causes them to stumble. Lord, I hope for Your salvation, and I do Your commandments. My soul keeps Your testimonies, and I love them exceedingly. I keep Your precepts and Your testimonies, for all my ways are before You.

Psalm 119:161-168

There is a movement in Christianity that believes God saved the church to be positive thinkers. Does that mean Christians should walk around with a smile on their faces in the midst of suffering, persecution, and affliction? Should Christians believe evil does not exist? Did God save the church so it could become the center of attention for the human race? Although these absurdities are ridiculous, human beings, generally speaking, think they are very important.

Pride is the reason people think they are so important. Psychological foolishness is the reason people think they are so smart. Material possessions tend to inflate the human ego thus making them think they have something they really do not have. In this confusion is a blatant assumption that autonomous man can save himself. The Bible teaches and history has proven that mommy and daddy cannot save themselves let alone their children. Hidden in the crevices of a dark mind is the idea that God saves the aristocracy to rule over the rest of mankind. Those aristocrats by their own definition believe they are the privileged ruling class. These exercises demonstrating the massive chaos among the human race in general and the church in particular could continue on and on. God saves His church because of His lovingkindness, grace and mercy. God sent his Son to suffer and die for the church. He sent His Holy Spirit to enable His church to believe.

The secular culture has always been in conflict with the sacred church. During the 20th century the materialism of modernity and all her children tried to persuade the church to follow the gods of modernity. Modern man lives in a world that naturalizes all of life and existence. In the 21st century the individualism of postmodernity prevails on the church. The postmodern man lives in a world that neutralizes moral standards and leaves no hope for the future. All theories of interpretation are autonomous to the interpreter. If postmodern preachers talk like a sophist using gobbledygook, it probably is gobbledygook.

Mikhail Gorbachev and Boris Yeltsin were leaders in the Soviet Union during the latter years of the 20th century. One political ally of Mikhail Gorbachev once said that Boris Yeltsin was a "political animal." The accusation was that Yeltsin pursued postmodern ideas and that those ideas made no distinction between good and evil. I'm not so sure that Yeltsin was a postmodern disciple, but I'm sure that the postmodern mindset had influenced him. The postmodern mindset has had and is still having a tremendous influence in our daily lives. It is like a cancer. It very quietly eats away at reality until finally that which is really real is no longer on the table for discussion. The postmodern concept affects every person in western civilization every day. Postmodernity changed the way people formulate world views that are contrary to rational intelligence.

Historical revisionism was popularized by postmodernity, thus distorting the truth of historical development. Revisionist history is the re-writing of history with the conspicuous absence of original sources. When people write history without the presuppositions of biblical ethics and norms, sinners that they are, they tend to distort history by imposing a personal relative ideal. They have a hostile disposition towards the God of history, which clouds their thinking and the interpretation of true history.

Literary deconstructionism is the postmodern tool to change communicating truth to mere communication. In simple language it teaches that words are meaningless, but those words can have meaning if the reader re-constructs the text according to his or her own world view and understanding of life. It basically discredits the structural foundations for established patterns of literary forms. God gave us language to have fellowship with Him and other rational creatures. We must use language wisely, prudently, and carefully.

I have referred to aesthetic annihilation as the death of reasonable art forms. The postmodern effect on aesthetics and the arts is the absolute distortion of reality. For example, the entertainment industry produces movies that use unrealistic characters with powers of creation and annihilation. The fascination with gory, angry, and murderous characters that have unrealistic forms consume the industry. Reasonable aesthetics ought to engage the mind to perceive beauty, peace, and harmony.

I'm not sure how to tell God's people to stand against the evils of postmodernity, except to use the biblical language which the Psalmist used, "I hate and abhor lying" (Psalm 119:163). The Lord said through the mouth of the prophet Zechariah, "Give judgment in your gates for truth, justice and peace...And do not love a false oath. For all these are things that I hate" (Zechariah 8:17).

A liar is one who is at war with reality. In contrast to the liar the Psalmist says those who love the law have great peace. It may sound contradictory when the Psalmist says "those who love the law have great peace." Psalm 120 describes the Christian living in this world. The Psalmist said, "My soul has dwelt too long with one who hates peace, I am for peace, but when I speak, they are for war" (Psalm 120:6-7). Jesus clarifies the confusion. Jesus said, "These things I have spoken to you that in Me you may have peace. In the world you will have tribulation..." (John 16:33).

When we die the Word of God declares we enter into peace (Isaiah 57:2), but while we live as pilgrims on this earth, the peace of Christ must enter into us. There is a sense in which Christians have peace, but they live in a battlefield. The battlefield encompasses all of this life because of sin. The postmodern concept is a perfect example. The battles rage over history because revisionist history is more of a falsehood than it is truth. Where there is a lie, there will always be a battle. The field of literature is under severe attack because the postmodern interpretation is more of a falsehood than it is truth. The average person may realize the most powerful enemy they have is in the world of aesthetics and art, because Hollywood art today is more of a falsehood than it is truth.

If Christians want peace with God and man, they must come to hate and despise falsehood, but come to love the Word of God in its fullness. If Christians want objectivity or to put it another way if they want one standard upon which to measure life as it really is and ethics as they are bound to be, then God's people must come to hate and despise falsehood, but come to love the Word of God. If they want coherency and harmony while they live in this lively battlefield, then they must come to hate and despise falsehood, but come to love the Word of God.

There is no such thing as neutrality when it comes to peace and war. There is no such thing as neutrality when it comes to love or hate. The Lord Jesus Christ said, "No one can serve two masters; for either he will hate the one and love the other, or he will hold to one and despise the other" (Matthew 6:24). If you love good, then by necessity you must hate evil. If you love truth, then by necessity you must hate falsehood. Love and hate ascends or descends, so it is measured by degrees, but there is no neutrality. The more a believer loves the Word of God, to that same degree the believer will hate falsehood.

If Christian believers really love the Word of God, they have true Christian peace. Christian peace does not depend on smiles, perceived happiness, and carnal pleasure. Christian peace is measured by how much Christian believers love God. If they love God, they will love His ultimate authority demonstrated in the Word of God. "Great peace have they who love Your law, and nothing can make them stumble" (Psalm 119:165). In the context of this Psalm, the "law" refers to the whole counsel of God, not merely the Ten Commandments. The Word of God is absolute. Without it there can be no peace.

We live in a society that is postmodern in every way. It denies the true peace, which comes from God. God the Father is called the God of peace (Hebrews 13:20). God the Son is called the Prince of peace (Isaiah 9:6). God the Holy Spirit is called the Spirit of peace (Ephesians 4:30).

23. Authority of God's Word

Let my cry come before You, O Lord; Give me understanding according to Your Word. Let my supplication come before You; Deliver me according to Your Word. My lips shall utter praise, for You teach me Your statutes. My tongue shall speak of Your Word, for all Your commandments are righteousness. Let Your hand become my help, for I have chosen Your precepts. I long for Your salvation, O Lord, and Your law is my delight. Let my soul live, and it shall praise You; And let Your judgments help me. I have gone astray like a lost sheep; Seek Your servant, for I do not forget Your commandments.
Psalm 119:169-176

The ultimate authority for the soul of man is the triune God. He has revealed everything necessary for faith and life in the Word of God. Therefore, the Word of God becomes the ultimate authority for God's children. Psalm 119 was obviously written before the Bible was in its completed form as we know it today. Critical scholars try to date it, but they are merely educated guesses and opinions. My opinion for what it is not worth, is that David wrote this Psalm. If the Psalm is dated in David's lifetime, the only Bible he had was the first five books of the Bible consisting primarily of the Law. The Psalmist used other terms to describe the full counsel of God. The Bible in its full and complete form is specifically for believers. Jesus distinguished believers from unbelievers. He explained in the gospel of John. Jesus was in the temple area teaching when the Pharisees confronted Jesus, accusing Him of being a false witness. His response was, "You know neither Me nor My Father. If you had known Me, you would have known My Father also" (John 8:19). The "if" clause is important because it brings to question the credibility of the relationship the Pharisees had with the God they professed to worship. The following is the inspired record of Jesus explaining how to distinguish believers from unbelievers.

> "I know that you are Abraham's descendants, but you seek to kill Me, because My Word has no place in you. I speak what I have seen with My Father, and you do what you have seen with your father." They answered and said to Him, "Abraham is our father." Jesus said to them, "If you were Abraham's children, you would do the works of Abraham. But now you seek to kill Me, a Man who has told you the truth which I heard from God. Abraham did not do this. You do the deeds of your father." Then they said to Him, "We were not born of fornication; we have one Father—God." Jesus said to them, "If God were your Father, you would love Me, for I proceeded forth and came from God; nor have I come of Myself, but He sent Me. Why do you not understand My speech? Because you are not able to listen to My Word. You are of your father the devil, and the desires of your father you want to do. He was a murderer from the beginning, and does not stand in the truth, because there is no truth in him. When he speaks a lie, he speaks from his own resources, for he is a liar and the father of it. But because I tell the truth, you do not believe Me. Which of you convicts Me of sin? And if I tell the truth, why do you not believe Me? He who is of God hears God's Words; therefore you do not hear, because you are not of God." (John 8:37-47)

Against the assumptions of the liberal theologians who do not believe the Bible is the Word of God, read this text again. Every human belongs to the household of Satan or the household of God. Satan's children will not believe the Word of God. Unbelievers will not be persuaded the Bible is the Word of God. However, believers are persuaded by the power of God's Spirit that the Bible is the Word of God. The Holy Spirit reveals the truth and reality in the Word of God. The child of God will not grow weary of hearing God's Word. He or she would never say, "God's Word is redundant." However, the authority of God's Word is self-evident.

God's Word is supernatural in its content.
God's Word is sufficient in its teaching.
God's Word reflects the majesty and aseity of God.
God's Word is not contradictory in any of its parts.
God's Word reveals the only way of man's salvation.
God's Word discovers the meaning of faith and life.
God's Word reflects the perfection of all its parts.

The Psalmist was not ashamed to call on the Lord. If the Word of God means anything to Christians, they should call on the Lord personally and passionately.

The evidence for belief that the Word of God is true will be reflected in our actions. If Christians actually believe that God is the almighty creator, that He upholds and sustains what He creates, and that God provides for His creation, then God's people should desire His Word personally and passionately.

For unbelievers, the Word of God is an intolerable set of rules that must be destroyed and replaced with the lies of Satan, which will lead one to death and eternal punishment. Even so, unbelievers should be encouraged to read it because from it they may see their sin and need for a Savior. The Word of God reveals the way of salvation.

The Word of God is for God's people, for it speaks to them and they gladly believe it. For God's people His Word is a treasure - a treasure that will lead one to life and eternal praises to the Lord God Almighty.

About the Author

Martin Murphy has a B.A. in Bible from Columbia International University and Master of Divinity from Reformed Theological Seminary. Martin spent nearly thirty years in the class room, the pulpit, the lectern, the study, and the library. He now devotes most of his time consolidating academic and practical gains by writing books. He and his wife Mary live in Dothan, Alabama. He is the author of twelve Christian books.

The Church: First Thirty Years, by Martin Murphy, 344 pages, ISBN 9780985618179, $15.95. This book is an exposition of the Book of Acts. It will help Christians understand the purpose, mission, and ministry of the church.

The Dominant Culture: Living in the Promised Land, by Martin Murphy, 172 pages, ISBN 970991481118, $11.95. This book examines the culture of Israel during the period of the Judges. It explains how worldviews influence the church and it reveals biblical principles to help Christians learn how to live in the culture.

My Christian Apology, by Martin Murphy, 98 pages, ISBN 9780984570874, $7.95. This book investigates the doctrine of Christian apologetics. It explains rational Christian apologetics.

The Essence of Christian Doctrine, by Martin Murphy, 200 pages, ISBN 9780984570812, $12.95. This book was written so that pastors and laymen would have a quick reference to major biblical doctrines. Dr. Steve Brown says it was written, "with clarity and power about the verities of the Christian faith and in a way that makes a difference in how we live."

Return to the Lord, by Martin Murphy, 130 pages, ISBN 9780984570805, $8.95. This book is an exposition of Hosea. The prophet speaks a message of repentance and hope. Hosea's prophetic message to Old Testament and New Testament congregations is, "you have broken God's covenant; return to the Lord." Dr. Richard Pratt said, "We need more correct and practical instruction in the prophetic books, and you have given us just that."

Theological Terms in Layman Language, by Martin Murphy, 130 pages, ISBN 9780985618155, $8.95. This book was written so that simple words like faith or not so simple words like aseity are explained in plain language. *Theological Terms in Layman Language* is easy to read and designed for people who want a brief definition for theological terms. The terms are in layman friendly language.

Brief Study of the Ten Commandments, by Martin Murphy, 164 pages, 9780991481163, $10.95. This book will help Christians discover or re-discover the meaning of the Ten Commandments.

The Present Truth, by Martin Murphy, 164 pages, ISBN 9780983244172, $8.95. Each chapter examines a topic relative to the Christian life. Topics such as church, sin, anger, marriage, education and more.

Doctrine of Sound Words: Summary of Christian Theology, by Martin Murphy, 423 pages, ISBN 9780991481125, $16.95. This is a book of Christian doctrine in topical format. It covers a wide range of theological topics such as, the triune God, creation, providence, sin, justification, repentance, Christian liberty, free will, marriage and divorce, Christian fellowship, et al). There are thirty three topics beginning with "Holy Scriptures" and ending with "The Last Judgment." It is a systematic theology for laymen based on the full counsel of God.

Friendship: The Joy of Relationships, by Martin Murphy, ISBN 9780986405518, 48 pages, $6.49 . This is the kind of book that friends give each other and share the principles with each other. If friends do not feel comfortable sharing these relationship principles with each other, the friendship may not really exist. Friendship involves a relationship of distinction. It is a relationship that respects the dignity of another person. The Bible teaches a different version of what it means to be a friend than the popular culture teaches. There are many occasions when friends say they are friends, but they are not friends. "Even my own familiar friend in whom I trusted, who ate my bread, has lifted up his heel against me" (Psalm 41:9). A true friend will endure and sacrifice for a friend. "A friend loves at all times" (Proverbs 17:7) and "there is a friend who sticks closer than a brother" (Proverbs 18:24).

www.ingramcontent.com/pod-product-compliance
Lightning Source LLC
Chambersburg PA
CBHW061728020426
42331CB00006B/1145